Primary Spe

PRIMARY SPEECH

SPEECH

A Psychology
of Prayer

ANN and
BARRY
ULANOV

John Knox Press
ATLANTA

ACKNOWLEDGMENTS

Grateful acknowledgment is made to the following publishers for permission to quote from the works cited:

To Harcourt Brace Jovanovich, for lines from *East Coker* by T. S. Eliot, from *Four Quartets*.

To Oxford University Press for lines from "The Leaden Echo and the Golden Echo" and "Carrion Comfort" from *The Poems of Gerard Manley Hopkins*.

To Pantheon Books, a Division of Random House, Inc., for lines from "A Vision of Prayer," from *Basic Verities* by Charles Péguy, translated by Ann and Julian Green, copyright 1943.

We acknowledge with particular thanks the help given us by Staley Hitchcock, who is not only a splendid typist but in his decipherings of our manuscripts is gifted with second sight.

Unless otherwise indicated Scripture quotations are from the Revised Standard Version of the Holy Bible, copyright, 1946, 1952 and ©1971, 1973 by the Division of Christian Education, National Council of the Churches of Christ in the U.S.A. and used by permission.

Library of Congress Cataloging in Publication Data
Ulanov, Ann Belford.
    Primary speech.

    Includes bibliographical references.
    1. Prayer—Psychology. I. Ulanov, Barry.
II. Title.
BV225.U4   248.3'2   81-85328
ISBN 0-8042-1134-5   AACR2

Printed in the United States of America

John Knox Press
Atlanta, Georgia 30365

For Alexander, Katherine, Nicholas, and Anne

Preface

We all speak many languages. We speak in neat sequences of cause and effect, knowing what we want to say and saying it with something like a measurable logic. We speak in quantum jumps, leaping or lurching from point to point, never quite sure of what it is we want to say but trying nonetheless to say it. We speak in signs and symbols. We speak with knowing indirection and we speak evasively, sometimes knowing how much we want to dodge confrontation, sometimes not at all aware of how hard we are to track down or even to follow. But in all these worlds of discourse, of thought and feeling, no language is quite so fundamental or so important as one that many of us are not even aware that we speak, the language of prayer.

Prayer starts without words and often ends without them. It knows its own evasions, its own infinite variety of dodges. It works some of the time in signs and symbols, lurches when it must, leaps when it can, has several different kinds of logic at its disposal. The point is that it knows what it is doing even when what it knows is that it does not know what it would like to know. Prayer's world is a world of honesty, where we face ourselves and for as long as we can remember — and perhaps even longer — have been facing ourselves.

Prayer, as this book contemplates it, is primary speech. It is that primordial discourse in which we assert, however clumsily or eloquently, our own being. If we are ever honest with ourselves, it is here that we must be, though we are often not sure about who it is that we are talking to or how well we are talking or that we are even talking. Sometimes the honesty comes because we are confident that nobody can overhear us, not the God in whom we have such shaky faith or no faith at all, not anybody we know, perhaps not even ourselves as we grunt or moan or shout or sob our prayers. Sometimes the honesty comes because we do know who it is that is listening, because we feel sure that there is a listener somewhere in us or outside us, because we know from experience that what we have said in prayer, or not quite said but somehow expressed, has been heard. Prayer, we have come to understand, is primary speech, though we do not call it that and may be surprised to find it so defined.

In this book, some of the consequences of identifying prayer as primary speech are examined. The examination results, we think, in a psychology of prayer. It is not a systematic psychology with all its parts in place, for the world of prayer — happily, we think — does not lend itself to that sort of scientific or pseudo-scientific analysis. But it is a world in which the imagination has a central role and where, as a result, the insights of those great specialists of the imagination, the masters of depth psychology, are particularly useful. Their perceptions sit side by side here with those of the acknowledged experts in prayer — theologians, mystics, poets, philosophers, some from religious communities, some from worlds that do not acknowledge any connection with conventional religion, much less with what we insist upon calling prayer.

We have made the connections here and have felt we must make the connections. For if prayer is primary speech then it is everybody's speech and even those who do not know they speak that language and want nothing to do with anything that can be called prayer have something to say to us about this subject. Prayer, we are saying, is a matter of taking what is there, taking ourselves, taking our world, and making what we can of both with the help of a magnificent tradition and a new richness of insight.

Take what is there. That, in a very few words, is what this book is about. To live in the fearful conflicts and uncertainties of our time, we are saying, we must take ourselves as we find ourselves and where we find ourselves and make the best of it all. That means, as we have tried to make clear, accepting the facts about ourselves — our fears and fantasies, our aggressions, our desires, our sexuality, our spirituality.

That means seeing what is positive, as well as what is not, in our reality. That means accepting our reality and it means accepting and making full use of prayer as a guide to understanding our reality, even if that use is very different from what we have thought was the proper way to use prayer. It means seeing that prayer really is our primary speech.

To facilitate that seeing, we have added to our text a brief appendix on the art of prayer, listing the names of composers, poets, painters, and sculptors whose work we have found particularly effective in stirring the movements of primary speech, and a very full set of footnotes. The footnotes are designed not only to identify sources but also, wherever possible, by quotation, paraphrase, or commentary, to offer the wisdom of major authorities in prayer. Prayer, as the words so often demonstrate, is where wisdom finds a special dwelling place.

A. U.
B. U.

Contents

One	Primary Speech	1
Two	Prayer and Desire	13
Three	Prayer and Projection	27
Four	Fantasy and Prayer	35
Five	Living with Fantasy	45
Six	Fear and Prayer	51
Seven	Prayer and Aggression	63
Eight	Sexuality and Prayer	73
Nine	Praying for Others	85
Ten	Answers to Prayer	99
Eleven	The End: Transfiguration	115
Appendix		129
Notes		137

Chapter One
PRIMARY
SPEECH

Everybody prays. People pray whether or not they call it prayer. We pray every time we ask for help, understanding, or strength, in or out of religion. Then, who and what we are speak out of us whether we know it or not. Our movements, our stillness, the expressions on our faces, our tone of voice, our actions, what we dream and daydream, as well as what we actually put into words say who and what we are.

To pray is to listen to and hear this self who is speaking. This speech is primary because it is basic and fundamental, our ground. In prayer we say who in fact we are — not who we should be, nor who we wish we were, but who we are. All prayer begins with this confession.

Prayer is primary because this speech of confession comes first in any act of praying, whether we know it or not. In prayer we speak out of our "flesh," the ground of all our experience, collecting into awareness what our self is saying, both what we know and what we do not know. Augustine says that our prayers have a voice of their own, quite apart from our own voice.[1] God hears all the voices that speak out of us — our vocal prayer, the prayer said in our minds, the unvoiced longing rising from our hearts, the many voices of which we are not conscious but which cry out eloquently. The God to whom we pray came to us in the flesh and speaks to us now in the flesh of our human self and our world. And even if we do not pray to the God of Scripture or traditional religion, still, every time we call for help or understanding from forces beyond us, we pray to something that one way or another seems to respond to us in terms of our humanity.

Prayer's first act of confession is the discovery of this primary speech. We begin to hear the self we actually are emerging out of our shadow selves, our counterfeit selves, our pretended selves. We become aware of what is in us, the best and the worst. Our best parts, if left unlived, can be as poisonous as our worst, if left unhealed. In this first act of collecting and recollecting we discover the fine impulses we failed to act upon, the kind words we left unsaid, the ambitions we left undared.[2] And we discover our worst sides: our envy of others' success, our reluctance to give, our refusal to be fully present to others, our many large greeds. Above all, we discover our fears — the fear to risk, to love, to submit, the fear to lead, to stand out and be seen. We have no nerve of failure. So we play it safe and live in the shadows rather than the light.

If we can let ourselves go in prayer and speak all that is in our minds and hearts, if we can sit quietly and bear the silence, we will hear all the bits and pieces of ourselves crowding in on us, pleading for our attention. Prayer's confession begins with this racket, for prayer is noisy with the clamor of all the parts of us demanding to be heard. The clamor is the sound of the great river of being flowing in us. This is what depth-psychologists call "primary-process thinking," that level of our psyche's functioning that leads straight to the workings of our souls.[3]

Prayer is also primary in the sense that its speech includes this mental process, this unconscious voice that exists in us from the very beginning, from the moment of birth. This primary speech does not begin with words, but starts much earlier in human life, with instincts and emotions and with an infant's first discriminations of value. They occur when a baby discovers that the flow of milk from its mother's breasts is or is not accessible, is or is not plentiful. Concepts of "good" and "bad" take shape at that point, as Melanie Klein has wisely observed.[4] Prayer often starts in much the same way. We are pushed to our knees by an instinct of fright, a desperate cry for help, or an overflowing need to reach out to something we sense is there. John of the Cross talks about God's response to the beginner in prayer as a mother to her nursling.[5] We are fed and comforted with sweet sensations. We are held and carried along by a presence so much larger than our own. Or, we feel left, empty, dropped in the dark, unfound by that someone or something toward which we are reaching blindly. Below the level of consciousness, like the infant with its fragile nascent ego, we begin to form concepts of "good" and "bad" in prayer. We begin to create value out of our experience as well as to find it there, given us, for our discovery.

The infant asks for help, blessing those who bring it, and condemning those who refuse it. The blessings and condemnations are clearly not verbal. They are often the merest signals of pleasure or disquiet, but they are unmistakable. From the gurgles of joy or the cries of outrage we can hear a system of speech falling into place. We cannot fail to notice that this youngest kind of being has begun to respond to its world and to find in it something good and bad. So it is with the person newly come to prayer. Below the threshold of words, discriminations of value begin to happen. Reaching in the dark, we sense response and fill up with this blessing experience, returning to find it again, experiencing it now as good. We fill up with gratitude. Remaining lost in the dark and hearing only our own angry cries, we feel emptied, diminished. If we allow ourselves to hear this level of speaking which is there in our praying, the filling and emptying moments, we will soon recognize that prayer is a noisy and vigorous business, not unlike the infant's first divisions of the world into large "goods" and "bads." A spiritual world begins to take rudimentary shape. The resources of our infancy, those earliest discriminations of value, get translated into the motions of prayer.

The language of primary-process thinking is not verbal. It comes in pictures and emotion-laden wishes and is private to ourselves, not really communicable, even though we all share in it. This language speaks our secrets, even those we keep from ourselves. This inner language of images and values feeds our outer language of words. When a child begins to teach itself the complex system of signals and expressions that is language, it is also teaching itself a value system. The child who has words has a way of responding in detail to everything and everyone around it. Distinctions can now be shaded and lightened. It is possible to say things, not merely to others, to get what one wants or to refuse what one does not want, but to oneself.

A child learning to talk and to hear what is being said is a person beginning to recognize what it means to be a person. Consciousness as we understand it is developing. But this is not the very beginning of consciousness or the first speech the child has spoken or listened to. The first speech is the language of instinct, emotion, and images. Primary speech is the set of responses that the infant feels and expresses as it deals with the central fact of its early days — the presence or absence of its primary food. What is so remarkable is that the new being, so very recently arrived at being in the world, can do something with those responses, can react and tell us about its reactions, and can and will attempt to influence our reactions. Primary speech is a spectacular reaching out on the part of new being to tell us that it is new being, that it is here, that it *is*.

Prayer reflects the mixture of the first primary speech of image and emotion with the words we acquire to express them. Our words act like a net that gathers in the numerous images that constantly flow through us from different sources. In prayer, the images of primary process rise to the surface so that we can inspect them. We find personal images that keep running through our minds — bits of the day just ended, or our more remote past, a quarrel or irritation, a gray feeling that reminds us of childhood winter afternoons. We discover images that shape our sense of ourselves — feelings that we are fat or in some other way out of shape, pictures of ourselves as dumb or foolish, or, on the other side, inflated images of ourselves saying the clever words or outfoxing a rival or being so powerful or helpful that everybody must turn to us. We find images flooding into us from our daily world. Images of crowds, of traffic. Images of nature — a field, a bird, dogs. Images from films, newspapers, radio, television — hostages held captive, mothers with starving babies, invading soldiers, frightened people. Images of horror and suffering. Frivolous images of cheap entertainment loud in the mind's ear. Fearful images of exploding volcanos, radioactive fallout, an earth exhausted of its air and water. Images of our time in history enter our prayer, shape it, crowd it, demand to be heard and taken into account. Prayer is not an escape from the world but an entrance into it. We become conscious in prayer of how much the world is with us and how much we are in the world.

Prayer opens a door to unconscious images, too, images we did not know we possessed. We may remember dreams or fantasies and be shocked suddenly to realize how frequently that particular image has been with us. We discover how often we dream of being left out of the in-group back in school, or of being chased by a nameless threatening pursuer. We see how many times we have felt suffocated as if there were no space to be or to become, how often that fear of being empty at the center has been there at the bottom of everything. Prayer is no escape from delusion or illusion. Prayer wakes us up to the terrors that frighten us from inside and to the primary life that flows in us, too — the drive to be, to be satisfied and full of gratification — a life, we see now, that often frightens us with its intensity.[6]

When we pray to be cured of a minor pain or a major one, a passing physical difficulty or one that might be very serious indeed, we have little trouble admitting what it is that is bothering us. We may be shy about some of the details, uneasy about dwelling on an unbecoming symptom such as a swollen face resulting from a toothache or a disfiguring skin infection. We may be wildly fearful, projecting the grim possibilities of this bump or that, this a-rhythmic disturbance or that. But in our prayer, we usually let it out, if not altogether openly to ourselves, then in some way or another to the clear inspection of whoever it is that may be listening — God or the collective unconscious or whatever strange gathering of powers to whom we have decided to entrust our miseries.

When the subject is moral failure, real or imagined, or harrowing dream-images or lustful or greedy wishes, we are not equally forthcoming. We want to hide it, even in the shadows of inner confidence where we ask the object of our prayers to look carefully to find out what is wrong with us and take care of it.

If we are guilty of ruthless ambition in our work which pursues us in those private moments of prayer where primary speech takes over, we begin the elaborate game of suppression that ends in silence, or worse, dishonesty about ourselves, even to ourselves. If we are beset by frenzied or ridiculous sexual fantasies which, however foolish or offensive to our sense of the rational and the proper, still somehow fascinate us, we feel the need to disown them. Or we put them in a secret corner of our memory where nobody else will know about them, except perhaps our great confederate in such picture-making, our inner officer who is in charge of Guilt. If we are furious with our wives or husbands or children or somebody with whom we work, we build up once again the apparatus of denial. We cannot, in most cases, altogether suppress the anger any more than we can completely get rid of the sexual fantasies or the power drives that pursue us, but we can all too easily transform all of it into an attack on ourselves.

If prayer is, as we believe, primary speech and the most direct line of communication we have to our interior reality, then every denial of that reality, every judgment or retreat from it that shuts off access to it is a serious diminishing of ourselves. It is, in fact, a kind of refusal to be. Far from achieving moral stature, we begin a kind of moral torture, for it is not the inordinate ambition or power drive, the lubricious sexuality, or the hostility toward those around us that makes us small, but the refusal to admit its existence in us.

Few experiences are so important in the development of the language of primary speech as those of admission. We must own up, stop denying, say yes to the moral bumps and rhythmic breaks and disfigurations just as we do to the physical. We do not necessarily bless them this way, or even fully support them. We simply accept the fact that they exist in us, that they are part of us, and that they cannot be denied. We do not have to make a public show of them any more than we have to go out and display our physical disfigurations to everybody who knows us. But to ourselves, to our inner selves, in the language of primary speech, we must make the first acknowledgment that matters. These things exist. We will not turn away from them.

Unfortunately, there is a long and honorable tradition that tells us to deny them. Fear the tempting images and the haunting emotions, we are told. They represent the evil within us or that unspeakable terror outside, just waiting to get at us one way or another. Put all that beyond us, we are told by all sorts of good people, by the saints, by the time-honored precepts of the churches. Think of that dreadful kind of visitation that venerable old holy men had to put up with — naked dancing girls, beckoning figures of lust — in the deserts to which they had gone to free themselves from such horrors, in their monastic cells, scared, on their knees, before a sacred icon. Wasn't that the devil's way of tempting them? Or if not the devil, wasn't it a kind of rising from the depths of a long suppressed sexuality which the exaggerated rituals of religion had driven underground?

One way or another, it was clearly an ugly business. It shut the door, closed us off from ourselves by the moral equivalent of an ice-cold shower. And then what? Will it all go away? Will a fine orderly inner life ensue? Either with rational scourings of our foolish and sinful desires or with a heavy dose of scourging prayer, in which we invoke the shocked presence of an inner Guilt or outer God, will we put it all behind us? No!

We must somehow recognize the claims of reality in us, even those of us who are venerable holy men or women. Scolding or excluding parts of ourselves or shutting the door will not do. We must admit what is there. We should say to ourselves, for example, in the dancing-girl (or leering-lad) visitation, "What a remarkable thing! You're still alive, you old fool!" If a murderous anger assails us, directed at ourselves or others, we should not simply shut it off or be appalled. We should recognize, perhaps with awe, the intensity of feeling of which we are capable, and try to meditate on its meaning. Only *then* can we begin to use all that emotion effectively. And so, in the same spirit, with the other presences, ignoble in fact or fancy. They are part of our lives, the way we really are and the way we must be willing to see ourselves. The unspeakable haunting image, or desire, or feeling may be the only way our deep-down interior reality can speak to us. To refuse to listen is to assure ourselves of a terrible inner deafness. Not to see what is there, or to turn away from it as an impossible nastiness within ourselves, is to compound a difficult or frightening fantasy with a really destructive fiction, that we are not what we are. Somehow we think of ourselves (and religious people fool themselves this way again and again) as pure spirit, or we think we will become that kind of airy perfection if we work at it long enough and hard enough and suppress all that other ugly stuff. We want the spirit, not the flesh, or at least not *this* flesh!

The being, the force, the God who came to us in the flesh meets us there in the flesh of our experience, all of it, all of our self and our world, our conscious and unconscious lives. The spirit dwells in our flesh. Prayer is also primary in this sense, that being at last comes to be first. Finally, it is of primary importance among all the other images, images of God come into our prayer, brought from our worship, our culture, from wherever we locate our faith. These images also clamor to be heard. We may find a picture inhabiting us from our childhood of God as a friend when everyone else misunderstood us. We may find a childhood picture scarcely graspable in adult words of God as a strangely luminous force wrapped in a layer of gold leaf, one that we saw as a child in, of all places, an advertisement for cigarettes. Or, we may remember an image of a mysterious "something" that deeply impressed us with its superior authority, something that was not like anything human — a whirling form like a many-pointed rock or crystal lighted up from within.[7] We may find an image of God left over from a culture of another time — God as monarch or leader in battle. We may find images of God from the Bible — the shepherd, the mother nursing Israel, Jesus alone in Gethsemane, the stranger on the road with an uncanny presence. Or we may find images of deity characterized by their lack — a terrifying absence, an empty grayness, a black hole. We fear nothing will greet us from beyond, that there will be no representation of God at all. We hear only a silence made from the absence or denial of what we long for. God comes as void.

As the clatter settles and we collect the bits of ourselves into the speech of prayer, confessing them, knowingly speaking now with all the voices in us, these voices focus our attention on the one to whom we are speaking. All, like arrows, point to one aim: the Other who hears us. God thus becomes the primary focus of our prayerful primary speech.

Prayer is not just primary speech, image-laden and without sound. It is also ordinary human talk that addresses an other in familiar conversation about familiar things. Critics of prayer accuse those who pray of narcissistic withdrawal, of merely communing with their own wishes and fantasies, hiding from the tough problems and insoluble conflicts of the world.

Such critics must begin to pray. Then they will see how different the actual experience of prayer is from their reduction of it. Prayer is every kind of speaking. Its words and feelings and gropings are imbued with that intentionality which Husserl calls directional, a subject speaking towards an object and with an awareness of an object, however dim or fuzzy the awareness may be.[8] That object constitutes the subject as a conscious being — that is, ourselves, for in speaking to God in prayer we become aware of the self we are. We collect all the parts of ourselves into our awareness and our self gets bigger. Prayer to God, to the source of being, gives us more being, more self. But that is not the primary point of prayer; it is almost a by-product. The primary point is the other, the one we are seeking in our speech. The only way we know anything about God, Husserl tells us, is through praying. That is the mode of consciousness in which the object, God, appears to the subject, us.[9]

Prayer enables speech; it extends us beyond our known self into the unknown God. It sends our words toward this other whom we seek. We discover this way that what we thought was the seeking of our prayer is in fact a responding to the other's having sought us.[10] The questions of our prayer turn out to be answers to questions God has already put to us. The groping of our prayer turns out to be our fumbling response to God's initiative, to being touched by God. The speech of prayer, finally, is a series of replies to the word that God sends to us. Prayer is as far as one can get from the self-indulgence of narcissism. It is imbued with otherness; its very nature is otherly.

The otherness of prayer is shown to us in many ways, large and small. The small ways happen first. In the process of confessing who we are, we find ourselves addressed by the otherness within ourselves and the otherness within our world. We find ourselves met by others who do not see things the way we do, but insist on other points of view. For example, in prayer we cannot escape the memory of anyone's criticism of us. We must look at it from all sides and angles and cannot hide in a defensive reaction by turning it back on our accuser, saying it is his or her problem, not ours. In prayer we cannot avoid a dream or fantasy image that insists on our attention. We must inspect it and hear what it says about us. In prayer we discover odd coincidences and new insights that we know did not originate in ourselves. We cannot create or reproduce them at will. Being itself speaks to us in these events, and we listen. If we go on listening, we feel God pulling us, drawing us into another current, a larger, deeper, stronger one than our usual little force. Prayer tugs at us, pulls us into a life of abundance, of unceasing abundance. We become increasingly swept into the flowing of this other life through the small space of our self. Prayer takes us into our central self, and through it into the very origin of all self.[11] The speech of prayer tells us of the new life for psyche and soul that comes when we open the door to the one who stands there knocking.

It is at this point that our prayer takes shape. We begin a second set of responses to the feelings we have about being alive. These new responses are as central to our lives as those we developed as infants when we first began to distinguish between good and evil in our reactions to food. Then we created the sounds and gestures of physical appetite. Now, feeling the bite of spiritual appetite, we begin to create a vocabulary of hope. Prayer becomes systematic anticipation. Onto the present, which we know (or think we know) only too well, we graft the future.

If we have really listened to what has been brought to us in the peculiar accents of primary speech, we are well prepared to hope and to pray, to anticipate. If we have not listened, if we have denied rather than admitted to ourselves what we really do know about ourselves, our hopes will be meager or improbable. They will not be real anticipations at all, but rather a forlorn kind of daydreaming, whether small and unimaginative or bursting with inflated expectations. Such hope quickly becomes its opposite and the prayer that builds upon it leads only too quickly to depression or even despair. Anticipation requires admission. Hope depends upon our being willing to admit to being who we are. Prayer is willingness. We will not be given more if we refuse what has already been given to us.[12] We cannot expect anything to be added or changed in us if we are not willing to accept the facts about us and especially those facts, hidden away from everybody else, that only we know.

In prayer, even more than in the other ways we deal with our experiences, we must be honest with ourselves. The familiar world around us and the even more familiar world inside us simply must be granted their full reality. We must face the fact that we wish we had the riches someone else has — and the fact that we wish the other would lose those riches. We must acknowledge that we feel very frightened about whether we can really do our job. We must admit that we really loved a person whom we lost and not pretend we did not in order to ease the pain of losing him or her. Pleasure, pains, gnawing doubts, secret satisfactions or dissatisfactions about ourselves, difficulties or delights of any kind with ourselves and others must all be admitted. If we have come to that extraordinary world where otherness confronts us and we confront it, we must make ourselves ready for it in the only possible way we can do so — by offering it our own otherness.

Whatever we are or have been is our otherness. What distinguishes us from other people is what identifies us as otherly to them. That is a remarkable fact in itself, and to somebody, somewhere, at some time or another, a fascinating one. In each of our lives, there is at least one other person who will be intrigued by the otherness that we represent, if we really allow that otherness to be represented. It may be a parent, a teacher, a lover. It may be the most confirming of all presences, our sense of the ultimate other, recognizing in us our otherly qualities.

Each of us has some remarkable configuration of inner and outer qualities that no one else has. We learn about ourselves in our interior listening, in our responses to our own primary speech which then become our prayers of anticipation. Admitting ourselves as fully as we can to ourselves, in all our shades and tints of pain and delight, of goodness and not-so-goodness and less, we admit the future to ourselves. We give ourselves a basis for anticipation. We have a very substantial ground upon which to build our hopes. Our prayer has become an educated prayer.

What most of us find so hard is to believe that others exist who really are interested in us and in our otherness, even if it is only one other. There is a simple test which will confirm their existence. We must think hard about the people we have known, especially those we have loved or who have loved us, even the dull and boring people among them, the bedraggled ones, those of no pronounced character, no quickly attractive quality. Then, if we review our meetings with them, we will almost always find that at some time or another, in some moment of con-versation, some shift of facial expression or change of bodily posture, something somehow caught us. It may only have been a miniscule event, brief in time, barely identifiable in character. But there it was. It did exist. With the dull and the bedraggled, a sudden lifting of the oppression of mediocrity did occur. A minus quantity, a nonentity, became a person. With the loved ones, being was so wonderfully and vividly displayed that we felt overwhelmed by the generosity of presence.

The otherness that lives hidden in all of us, in the best of us, and in the least of us, suddenly sprang into open life. And so it is with any of us and with all of us. We can admit life into our being by admitting who we are and what we are to ourselves. We can admit being, as being admits us. And on the basis of that admission, we can hope and can anticipate whatever changes, whatever growth, whatever development we would like. We can pray.

The psychology of prayer we take up here looks at the issues the psyche faces when we pray. The psyche, the region of life's breath and mind, of conscious and unconscious mental processes, intermingles with the soul's life, the opening to being where God speaks softly to us.[13]

Anyone who prays must sooner or later stumble onto the issues that the following chapters address. We raise these issues for conscious inspection. We do not offer a psychological interpretation of them as a mental exercise once or twice removed from actual experience. Though useful in some settings, that is not helpful in entering the life of prayer.[14] There, too, many questions assault us. These questions are at the center of the following chapters. We believe only by going through them can our prayer be grounded in the flesh of human reality.

In other ages, prayer manuals offered counsel on how to remove distractions, avoid sexual images, exclude angry passions from prayer. Our time must go by another route, we believe. Being comes to us only through the incarnation. Thus our way to God, to discovering that God is already there with us, can only proceed in the flesh and through its passions, through our fullest humanity, what Christ promised as the abundant life.

Chapter Two
PRAYER
and DESIRE

All prayer begins with desire. Desire comes in many forms. At its best, desire in prayer is what Augustine calls an affectionate reaching out to God.[1] We long for contact, for connection at the center, that grounding that brings full-hearted peace of mind and soul. We want to be in touch with what lives within every thing that matters, with what truly satisfies, with what Kierkegaard sees as commensurate in its intensity of presence, with the intensity of our desire.

This desire that brings God down to the soul is like the thirst for the water of the spirit that Jesus reveals to the woman at the well.[2] It hides in lesser desires. The thirst is unquenchable, or at least seems to be. Most of us encounter its urgent demands hidden first in the upsurge of sexuality that comes with puberty. Nothing, it seems, will altogether appease our adolescent libido. No person, no physical experience, nothing seems to answer. There are ways of quieting the impulse. There are variously appealing kinds of transformation for that sudden abundance of energy — good works, good thoughts, cross-country runs, a thousand push-ups. But nothing will hold it all, and every act of suppression seems only to increase the energy and redouble its demands. There is good reason for it. The reaching out we do this way, in the throes of early sexual desire or any of the other demanding appetites, is a rehearsal and preparation for the great meeting with being which one way or another everything in our life strains to achieve. Desire is the motivating force that leads us toward that meeting and prayer the language in which that movement explains itself.

Prayers find their first motivations in desire. We pray for what we want. Like children who pray the weather will be fair enough so they can go swimming that afternoon, we pray as adults to get this job, this opportunity, that relationship. Desire in prayer goes on our whole life, as we pray the baby we carry will be healthy, that our sick child will recover health, that our parent may know an easy death, that our faith will be made stronger, that peace will come to our world, that we will do God's will.

Our life of desire prepares us for our life of prayer. We are blind in both. Desire is blind when it simply seeks quick and easy appeasement. Understanding is no part of such desire, nor are other people, except as useful pieces of the machinery of appeasement — someone to feed us, to caress us, to give our desire immediate satisfaction. Blind desire is impersonal even if it involves other persons; the other is there only for "me." Neither of us is there for the other or for the relationship. Self-gratification is all there is in blind desire.

But blind desire is not enough for most people. They may not be conscious of the limitations. They may even think of themselves as leading a trimphant life as lover or achiever of some kind or other. But somewhere in all of this there is a sense of inadequacy, of incompleteness, a desire for more than blind desire and its simple self-directed gratifications.

Somewhere there arises a determination to understand. Desire needs to be mediated by an other so that we can begin to see the desire and make it part of our self instead of blindly enacting it. The direct intervention of persons becomes a fundamental need. Human presence, and something more, beckons. Prayer is the language in which we respond to that movement from blind desire to the desire that seeks insight and relationship and at least the first glimpses of inner understanding.

For example, in prayer our very desires lead us to look toward the one who, in our child's view, may grant or withhold satisfaction. Prayer makes room for the child in us and allows us to grow up around and beyond that child. Prayers full of "I want" and "Please me!" lead to prayers involving other persons and, eventually, God's person. We pray for other people. We want good things to happen to them and bad things not to happen. We pray for help from other persons. Others enter our prayers and carry us into the personhood of God as we begin to see we are all motivated and held by something larger than self-gratification. A blind sexual desire can become part of the energy of love between two persons, first acting like an automatic impulse, catapulting one toward another person. In the same way our desires for our self expressed in prayers that begin in grossly self-centered concern lead us to the need and concern for others who change our sense of self and deliver us into God's self. When I pray for my friend, that friend's being touches my own being and all the voices of my being. I hear those voices and begin to understand them. My desire is no longer so blind. I can pray for others. I can even pray for my enemy. When I pray for my enemy, hard as that is to do, my enemy's grip on me loosens. While we do not fully understand all this change in ourselves, we sense it. Often now we pray for understanding: Let me see the way to go. Show me how. Shed light on this dark confusion so that I can find a way. We are praying for illumination and our prayers are beginning to be answered.

Prayer for understanding presupposes understanding. Prayer for the intervention of persons presupposes the existence of persons who will offer just such a presence in our lives. When desire leads to prayer — even the most crude and clumsily organized longing to find someone with whom to share and grow in that desire — grace has entered one's life. What we thought was simply blind desire starting out on its own, with nowhere in particular to go, turns out to be instead desire expressing a dim awareness of something already there. Instead of beginning a new line we discover we are already part of an old circle. But we do not discover this if we suppress or skip over any of our desires.

Desire in prayer shows itself in many forms. We go at God like a brass ring, wanting to catch deity and win the prize. We want so many prizes: fame, security, power. Often we want very good prizes: love, health, peace in the world, truth. We come to God in ways we are usually careful to conceal in our dealings with people. We do not say to a person, I want to be your friend because you are rich and may give me some of your money. But we do say to God, I pray to you because I want you to bless me, forgive me, help me, heal me. We do not openly show we want to marry someone because of what that person can then do for us — giving us safety, security, status, some leverage to wield against others.

We try to appear really interested in other persons for who and what they are in themselves.

With God, our desire is more naked, and rightly so. With no secrets, we come at God crudely, like beggars or greedy children. It is no good denying this or trying to mask it. We must see the crudeness and include it. God loves us in the flesh. Denying what God loves and died for is trying to go God one better, and only impedes our prayer. We must bring the crudeness along, too.[3] Even our greed, which God permits, may work for the good. It brings us urgently into prayer where God can get at us. Our greed then may be winnowed, chastened, refined.

For some of us, desire shows itself negatively, like the fear that Freud made us see hiding behind our wishes. We are afraid to pray; we doubt its venture; nothing seems to be there. At best, we wonder about it. At worst, we avoid it. It becomes a phobia. Here prayer begins in our talking about our doubts and fears.[4] Confusion, questions, even complaints start our conversation with God. We utter reproaches for God's absence. We dare God to be present. We feel blank and grope for the right words. No sense of God seems to be part of our experience. We sit in the dark. This is the kind of muddle that starts our conversation with God. We bring it all into our prayer as we should, for nothing which concerns us should be left out of prayer.

Desire may direct its force to the other to whom we pray. Desire may present itself as curiosity, or, in its deeper form, as yearning for knowledge. We want to know who this is to whom we speak.

Our praying, then, begins with a long series of questions: Who are you? Are you there for me? What are you like? What do you want from me? Do you have a face? Why do you allow suffering? How could you let such a terrible thing happen? Do you care about justice? Are you fair? Do you rule over history? Do you preside over the universe? What kind of God are you? Are you a person? How are you in Jesus? Will you show yourself to me? This sort of desire, formulated as a series of questions, may move us into what masters of prayer have for years called the second stage, meditation. We read about God in the Bible and in others' recountings of their direct experiences of God. We try to enter scenes in Scripture and penetrate their meaning by identifying with the characters. We reflect on divinity and try to arrange our imaginations to scrutinize this extraordinary, confounding mystery.

Desire leads each of us to begin praying from the premise of being, of who we are. What will sooner or later become our discipline in prayer starts in discipleship. We are students of being as we experience it. We notice what our own way is. We give our central attention to what we are saying and what we are already speaking for others to hear in our actions, words, and feelings. We can see the primary way in which we already are speaking to God and God is speaking to us. Prayer is taking notice of that speaking back and forth and joining our voice to it consciously.

In that act of taking notice, we receive one of the main by-products of prayer — an enlargement of the self God has given us. We consciously link up with what already speaks in us unconsciously. Our desire drives us further, to consent to go on, to open, to seek, to push outward, to want to be filled. Augustine put it succinctly in his observation that prayer is the construction of our desires.[5] God does not need to be told anything about what we need and want. Our words in prayer are not for God's instruction but our own. We discover this way what in fact we do desire, what we want to reach out to and love. Thus we come to hold in open awareness what before we had lived unknowingly.[6]

Surprises happen. We may discover we want more than we thought we dared. In the secret space of prayer, we may reveal to ourselves how much we want truth, beauty, love. In daily life, we usually hide from such desires, trying to protect ourselves from their urgency with the cynical argument that those are merely childish hopes that life correctly disillusions. We may discover desires we did not know about or knew only dimly, desires that if followed would take us far off the path we have so carefully constructed. We might have to change jobs, leave relationships, forsake our whole way of living to take up an entirely different one. Following desires does not, as critics might warn, necessarily lead to self-indulgence and all the hedonist sensations. Rather, it heads straight into the dangers of moral dilemma. The voice that God hears in prayer gets louder and louder for us if we go on praying. It may come to speak of a truth and a way of life that break sharply with the life we are living.

Prayer entered into seriously marks an unmistakable break with the way we have been living. It is never simply another happy little part of our lives, an attractive addition to the day or the night like a new car or a new dress or a fetching new way to prepare a soufflé.[7] Prayer is struggle. But prayer, following the dictates of an imperious desire, can become a voracious appetite and in its own time, at least, become all-consuming. Deal with it frivolously and all desire for it will disappear, or it will be converted into such a mere decoration in our lives that it might be better to give those middling energies over to a more easily satisfied appetite. A couple of set prayers on arising, a matching pair at bedtime, a fixed few in church, all barely attended to and finally reduced to empty rote repetitions, become less in our lives than breakfast coffee or nightly martini or the day's episode in the television soap opera.

The desire for prayer is the desire for a meeting with truth. It is the thirst for understanding which will give purpose to the boredom in which so many of us pass our working lives. It is the need to find sense beyond the easy answers of catechetics or any other form of natural theology, no matter how well-turned. The mind wants satisfaction in this desire, but not in itself alone. The disturbed body wants assuagement, but not a mere cessation of pain. The feelings want support and the emotions insist on some worthy object, but not in a world lived apart from the suffering body or clamoring mind. In the desire for prayer, a wrenching need for wholeness expresses itself. We want to live our metaphysics and to experience our beliefs. We want to know at first hand, and to know with all of ourselves, with our capillaries and our nerves and our muscles, to know in the rhythm of our blood and the openings and closings of our senses. We want to know directly and we want to know indirectly. We want to know in our waking moments and in our dreams at night when we are asleep. All of our life, when this desire commands us, must be an allegory of the knowledge it brings.

The knowledge we are seeking is not reducible to one set of facts, or one containable narrative, or even a plausible sequence of questions. Like the revelation a holy book or a holy life brings, it changes in meaning and understanding with the years and with cultures and with people. It means different things to us at different times in our lives. It is not reducible to formulas and constructions, for all the great truths it may contain.[8] It is the product of wisdom, not of scientific experiment, and therefore cannot find with each new perception a new formulation, such as $E = mc^2$, with which to gratify our hope for clarity. This knowledge is the knowledge of persons, both human and divine. And persons, as we all know, cannot be translated into fixed laws and algebraic summations.

Are we seeking something impossibly elusive, then? Are we looking for a paternal or maternal authority that will remove all care from our lives, all tension, all contradiction, without any of the difficulties that real family life presents? Is this simply a way to elude the problems and sufferings of maturity? Many thoughtful and wise people have insisted that the seekings of religion are illusions or delusions. The answers lie elsewhere, they have said, and for many they have said so with such persuasive eloquence and logic that the desire for prayer and its objects has been altogether erased or transformed into an ideological pursuit with very different solutions. Still others have attempted to mix seekings and solutions, bringing political and economic ideologies into partnership with religious doctrine. This will produce, they tell us, a liberating theology. In it, the motivating force of the spirit, religious belief, acts to change society, by violent revolution if necessary. All that is good in the world — as these thinkers understand goodness — works together for our good.[9]

And yet the desire for the other kind of knowledge persists among us, and not only for the knowledge but also for the direct experience of it in a wholeness that will bring all of the elements of our being together in understanding. The solutions of politics or economics and all the other disciplines that promise a totality of satisfaction, however important they may be, do not bring the satisfaction they promise. Or, even more remarkable, they do bring exactly those satisfactions — and yet they do not satisfy. Something else remains. We know what we do not know. We know that the desire is still there. We have another choice to make and so we move on to choose again.

Choice presents itself early on in prayer. We discover levels to our desire. We want lesser things; we want greater things. Smaller satisfactions beckon just as loudly at first as large contentments. Simple temptation tells us we have been setting our sights too low. We would settle for a lifetime of detective story thrillers and deny ourselves the nourishment of great novels and poetry. Spiritually, we fasten on junk food, giving up the sweet smell of a fresh cucumber or the juiciness of a ripe red tomato. We are choosing the polished inanities of pop, of muzak, not allowing ourselves to hear the startling sounds of a live string quartet or the astonishing arousal of first-rate jazz improvised on the spot. We prefer to stick to gossip with acquaintances and refuse the soul-stirring conversation of real friends. We flirt with passing sensations and avoid the transforming power of a sexual meeting in love. We reach out for inferior things this way and turn from the best. We may come then to refuse God's love. That is sin. And God's answering wrath is to leave us to our choice — to languish in these lesser pleasures since we have refused the greater things he offers.[10]

Prayer is the place where we sort out our desires and where we are ourselves sorted out by the desires we choose to follow. St. Ignatius Loyola developed his famous discipline in the life of prayer in this way. He tried different methods and judged their results by examining the feelings they left him with, seeing whether they steadied and increased his desire or left it wanting. The ones that gave him a quick euphoria and then a despondent feeling he soon abandoned. Those that yielded a steady and increasing sweetness he continued, building satisfaction on satisfaction.[11]

Desire leads to more desire. Prayer articulates our longing for a fullness of being, our reaching out of the mind for what is beyond it, and helps us find and love God and grow with our love. It is like the sun warming a seed into life, like the work of clearing away weeds and bringing water to the interior garden of St. Teresa's inspired imagery.[12] Prayer enlarges our desire until it receives God's desire for us. In prayer, we grow big enough to house God's desire in us which is the Holy Spirit.[13]

The greatest surprise of all is that the prayer that we thought to be our own activity, our own reaching out, reveals itself instead as God's Spirit moving in us. Our very desire to pray, that we took as our own, turns out to have a much larger source. We now see that the desires that we constructed through repeated efforts to pray, showing ourselves to ourselves, reflects God's desire moving us toward fuller being, toward the embrace of love. Our admission of desires into consciousness becomes an admission of divine presence. Our desire for something so utterly outside us mirrors the desire of that outerness to become our innerness. Our very doubts about prayer turn into a struggle to accommodate this foreign presence. Our curiosity and desire to know, we see, are the force of the knower seeking the known. What we thought was *our* prayer, *our* effort to pray, reveals itself as God's praying through us, the Spirit showing the things of Christ to us. We understand now why Christ insisted repeatedly that it was not he but God moving through him whose power people felt.[14] Our wanting to turn to God is God moving our will to turn to him. We are pulled into the primary speech of God, giving, receiving, and showing forth a constantly radiating force of relatedness. Our desire to pray has become a doorway into the heart of being.[15]

Grasping that prayer begins with a desire which we experience as our own and develops when we perceive even the desire itself as God's action in us, rearranges all the questions of discipline in the life of prayer. Discipline begins, as we must keep reminding ourselves, in our first being a disciple, a student, one who can learn, one who can be educated. By listening to the primary speech of our own prayer, we learn to begin where we are, finding the way that is entirely our own, no matter how awkward or stumbling or incomplete.[16] As the author of *The Cloud of Unknowing* so confidently assures us, we are not to worry about how to begin praying. God will show each of us our way. It is our peculiar, particular, freely given response that God wants, not some pre-packaged formula, some assembly line product.[17] The author of a little-known, infinitely wise essay, *The Art of Conversing with God,* puts it more daringly still:

> there is nothing which concerns you which does not appeal to His love . . . with you, in your little chamber, His thought is of you. All the designs of His Providence and of His love are concerned with your special interests. With you, and in the places where you are alone with Him, He is, so to speak, God for you alone. He is Almighty only to assist you. He is all loveable only to be loved by you and to invite your confidence; to give you the opportunity to tell Him what grieves you. . . . God wants you to tell Him all that afflicts you.[18]

Almost every kind of desire we have ever felt is now accessible to us if we recognize the presence that has come to us, the special concern for us and us alone that is speaking to us. Imagine all the intensity of feeling that we have ever known, every strand of our libido, no matter how slight, no matter how immense, suddenly concentrated and brought to attention upon us. That is what it is like to hear this voice within us and to heed it. That is what it means simultaneously to feel such a welling up of desire and to confirm its rightness for us in that speaking presence.

It takes a remarkable kind of willingness to go with desire, to move with the feeling of the spirit, in order to enable one to experience this meeting with life at the source. Reality constantly discourages even approaching the possibility of the experience. The ordinary encounters of our world diminish desire by trivializing it, reducing it again and again to the most trifling stirrings and satisfactions of the flesh. Persons as persons are not involved in such exchanges, in which words, gestures, physical feelings, human concerns, and the postures of love are reduced to a mechanical enactment at the emotional level of a cigarette or candy vending machine. But even this kind of dwarfing of the large impulses of desire to the mechanics of sexuality will not necessarily cut us off from the great presence that calls to us. It may require a deeper expression of our will. It may demand a more considerable concentration to hear and to gather in those feelings that have now been made so faint that they seem almost to have disappeared in the distance of an unrecoverable past. But it is always possible.

To come up to that formidable presence and to make ourselves ready for it always requires finding courage and discipline where they really live, at the center of our being. No matter how good or bad our lives may be, measured by the terms of a conventional morality, facing the divine is never a simple one-two-three operation. We do not accomplish it by any one method. Indeed, we may find ourselves deploring the tyranny with which "stages of prayer" have been used. A sequence of steps that was to guide the willing feet of desire is transformed through a sternly judging attitude into a series of condemnations of our inadequacies, insecurities, and incompleteness. (What, you are only at the first stage when you should be at the fourth?) We are not guaranteed satisfaction because we ourselves are giving satisfaction. Neither are we assured the grandeur of the presence, as so many of the inverted prophecies of the twentieth century seem to suggest, because we have fallen so low and have achieved such a dramatic squalor in our lives. We have become so completely the modern publican who, as Scripture assures us, clearly outranks the Pharisee. There are no guarantees, no assurances, no certainties in the ultimate precincts of desire except our own willingness. There is a special meaning to those constant injunctions to us to ask and to seek, with their unbelievable accompanying promise that we will receive, that we will find what we want. The special meaning is that we must be *willing* to ask, must be *willing* to seek.

To be willing is not to perform a prodigious act of will which strains every muscle of the spirit. To be willing means just what the words say, as the words of primary speech always do. Willingness is a going-with-desire. Willingness is moving with our own desires as they turn up, in the special ways they appear in our individual lives.[19] We can fantasize an encounter in outer space. We can dream of apparitions in church, over our roof, in some wonderfully designed grotto where nature is our grand accomplice. But our will and our understanding, shaped as they must be by the dimensions of our everyday reality, will never really accept the likelihood of that kind of meeting with the divine. We can satisfy desire only by meeting desire where we find it in the commonplace events and environments of our daily lives. We can achieve the fulfillment of the spirit only by a willingness to be ourselves, to respond to ourselves and through ourselves wherever we customarily find ourselves. If we are slow to move or to speak or to think things through, we must accept ourselves as slow. If we are quick and nervous by temperament and easily aroused, then we must accept those identifying qualities as our own.

We start in the flesh, with the flesh that we are, with the desires that we have, with our own way of loving, whatever it may be — felicitous, awkward, simple, complex, open, covert. We must find our own way, and having found it, accept it. We must be willing to take this kind of spiritual discipline with all its nagging reiterations of the ordinary facts of our life, but also with its equally insistent reminder that it is in that ordinariness that the Spirit will find us, that the Spirit has *already* found us. That is where we must begin listening. That is how we begin listening — and praying.

Consider time for example. All of us have trouble finding the time to pray. We solve the problem in different ways. We solve it best when we begin where we are, wherever we find ourselves praying or wanting to pray, for it is there that God is moving us, pulling us in to divine presence like fish on a line.

For some of us praying starts anytime, especially at unexpected times. It may be when we are jogging, doing exercises, or taking a bath. Or when we are cooking and sorting out ingredients, and playing around with fresh combinations, improvising new dishes. When we bend over our baby's crib. These are good times. Other good ones are when we ride the bus or the subway or work in the garden, or when we sit and stare into space, or when we lie down on the floor and feel its hardness under our backs. At such times we can go within and speak quietly to God. Some of us pray only when we cry or are desperate and afraid. Some of us set aside special times to pray, making a schedule. Some of us pray only in church, in the safety of set prayers or prayers vocalized for us. We must each begin in the way that comes to us, for in that way God is approaching us and knocking on our door.[20]

Attention to our own particular way makes new sense of the warnings the saints give us against starting a life of prayer and then stopping it. Teresa says that is more dangerous than not beginning at all, because then we fall from a greater height and hurt ourselves more seriously. Brother Lawrence says that not to keep going forward in one's spiritual growth is to go backward.[21]

We touch something hot when we begin to pray. We open to the primary speech emerging from our own depths. That is live material, full of potent images, impelling desires, poignant yearnings. To let this current freely into our awareness and then wander off and leave it unguided is like leaving one's house with the faucets on. They overflow and flood our space, or worse, seep unnoticed into the floorboards, starting rot. Jung tells us that "false unconsciousness" is dangerous.[22] To be aware of something and then to forget or deny that awareness sets up a division within us, puts a cover on growth that has already begun, causing twisted roots, gnarled stems, or broken branches.

One of the immediate effects of paying attention in prayer to our own desires — whatever they may be — is to experience changes in the desires. We feel them opening, steadying, and deepening. We have moments of uprush of desire, of going out of ourselves in acts of impulsive kindness, of a sudden talking to ourselves in ourselves where we divulge what we really think and feel, what really matters to us. Such moments of lavish expression are steadied and made more constant in prayer. They are disciplined, not in the sense of being restricted or held on a tight rein, but rather in the sense of being given their appropriate space. They no longer gush through us and disappear. Instead, they form a consistent flow of reliable good will toward ourselves and others. To start praying and stop halts this process of finding one's proper flow into life and runs the risk of losing connection to what matters in life. We may as a result no longer feel its astonishing stability.

If our desire to pray is in fact God's desire moving in us, we have touched the living Spirit. It is not just *our* primary speech we feel now but the primary presence of God acting within us.[23] This touch we feel is life itself reaching back to us. This is not a casual meeting in which we simply come and go. This is the center of everything for us. Here we are changed and made new without losing the old. We know bits of God's grace. To turn away delivers us into God's wrath. Although it is not a thundering condemnation, it is often silent but complete. We can no longer be reached or touched. God always respects our choice and leaves us to its consequences.[24] If we have put ourselves outside of life's flowing, we are stuck there. If our desire remains, no matter how weak, one prayer remains open to us. We can thank God for forgiveness and providing a way back.

Chapter Three
PRAYER
and PROJECTION

One of the ways back to God is through our projections. These images of God that we erect and pray to are of a God fashioned out of what we need and what we wish for. Our pictures of God come from the memories of real experience of dependencey on our parents and their responses to us. They come from our own fantasies about our parents' responses, in which we endow them with better or worse actions than they performed. Our pictures of God come from longings still with us, as for a strong ally who will protect and comfort us.[1] They are the result of impulses we cannot accept or escape in ourselves — usually of aggression and anger — that we delegate to this surrogate champion. We need someone larger than life who understands us and our fears. We want a God who will guarantee that life will be fair in the end, that the wicked will be punished and the good rewarded. Above all, we need an intermediary with the unknown. Our various pictures of God make this possible.

Freud attacks such pictures as deceptive.[2] There is no god except the one we make out of our wishes. Unwilling to see that these wishes originate in ourselves, we believe that they come from a being outside ourselves. Destroy these false gods, Freud urges, which merely reflect our own fears and hopes, merely embody our own wishes for consolation against life's harshness. They represent our dread of punishment for the aggression and envy we direct against our neighbor. In short, our images of God personify the unknown we fear. Through them, we attempt to control the unknown by turning it into a person like ourselves, only bigger, kinder, and all-wise. Smash those mirrors, says Freud, and grow up.

Many people take just that action and as a result cut themselves off from praying. If they do begin to pray, the images of God that appear to them seem false, all detours and illusions. Praying for them is contaminated with the fear of being childish, unrealistic, simple-minded. Prayer has become an embarrassment. So finally they do nothing, and they either suffer a lack where there once was the fullness of prayer or struggle with the reproach that the voiced longing within themselves is a stubborn, childish wish they long ago should have put behind them. They feel undermined, without a sure ground to stand upon or a place from which to grow.

Sometimes those of us left suspended in this place try to cover over the hole in the ground we feel beneath us. We are drawn into elaborating Freud's complaint against prayer as no more than the projection of our own wishes. Instead of reducing our images of God to personal wishes, we see them as the projections of groups and of society as a whole. God now personifies the social controls that operate among people, controls that have such a force that they take on a life of their own, like a separate being hovering above us. Or, God comes to be seen as a picture of the meanings we have poured into our sense of reality. These meanings are so important that they have been given a life of their own, with ritualized ways of connecting to it and special languages, usually drawn from the social sciences, for communicating with it. God is seen now as a social strategy, a ruling force. If the leaders of society draw on one picture of God, it is to instill obedience in their citizens. God becomes a tool of oppressive class struggle.[3]

Clearly none of these theories of God as projection can help us when we try to pray. Prayer is conversation with an other who is altogether different from us and our subjective needs and wishes and altogether present to us in its differences. That is what is so threatening about prayer — its speech is so personal, so intimate, and yet the conversation we conduct through it is open-ended. We confide our most private, our most guarded, our most secret wishes and fears and wait to hear, to learn, and to perceive the response that will come back to us. Our images of God begin this process of confiding. But the open-endedness of the conversation that follows soon goes far past those images and causes them to fade, even to break away completely. That is the purgation of prayer: we are stripped of our comforting intermediaries with the unknown. It is a bewildering and fearful process we have entered.[4]

In prayer we must begin where we are, with the images of the divine that we project and find ourselves projecting onto the unknown. God loves us in the flesh and part of our fleshly existence is in this psychological process where we take in parts of real people, fashioning from them images of their qualities and our feelings about them. Then those resultant projections seem quite outside ourselves, as if they had originated far from us and had no existence in us. This is one of the basic ways we interact with reality, through the process of taking in — introjection — and pushing out — projection.[5] It is not a process that is invariably the same. At different stages of our lives we experience the otherness of the unknown differently and construct different images of it.[6] We come to God at first through the way we need God to be.[7] Only slowly and with much experience of prayer can we allow God to come to us. Only then, after we have examined and recognized our introjections and projections for what they are, can we really hear another voice than our own.

One of the first tasks in prayer is to face the process openly, to notice what images we have of God and to welcome them into our awareness. Part of building this extraordinarily intimate relationship with the divine is finding what wishes and fears, hopes and desires impel us toward God. Recognizing positively, and without self-reproach, the needs in us which Freud diagnoses as childish and self-deluding, we can look at our images of the divine with new understanding. To begin with, we can search carefully within ourselves to see what it is we want to call this central embodiment of otherness.[8] Our images of God are our first names for God, those forms of address through which we approach the other as we feel the need for its otherness to come to us.

The primary speech of our prayer will surprise us here, for our conscious names of God, so often borrowed from our religious tradition, may contrast sharply with or even oppose the unconscious images of God that will rise to the surface if we lay ourselves open to them and welcome them.[9] We may start out praying to God as all-merciful, as our Sunday school lessons taught us to do, and be shocked to find entering our prayer a picture of God as nasty scorekeeper tallying up our faults in indelible ink. We may start praying by thinking we should not bring petty concerns to God, and discover to our amazement that we look upon God as a divine Santa Claus who will unpack his bag and deliver to us all the presents for which we have petitioned. We may begin praying to God as supreme goodness and grow anxious as we uncover a deep dread within us, of God as an alien force or an uncanny trickster or even a witch. We may find that our picture of the divine, which we thought of as so exalted and above human concerns, holds a curious resemblance to the totem animals of our early childhood —the bear, or giraffe, or pig that we carried around and slept with for so many years, that soothed our distress and helped us to sleep.[10] So equably did it withstand our angry attacks, so ready was it always to be loved, that we even loved the way it smelled, rank and dirty though it may have been. This relationship with God as childhood totem persists in the great saints' intimate lives with God. The saints arrive at their personal names for God in prayer — St. Teresa's "His Majesty," Brother Lawrence's "Benefactor," "Ever Present Lover," "King," Lady Julian's "Mother Jesus." These names embody the trust of that earliest confidence stretched to include the awe and force of the saints' encounters with the mystery of the divine.[11]

All of us need to find and shape our name for God from our own encounters with the mystery, however large or small these meetings may have been. In our language and images we recognize that all this may change with the years, the kinds of encounter, the depth of penetration of the mystery, even the names and images themselves. We see the great range in the theologies — the philosophical name of God as "Perfect Reason," as "Being Itself," the political name of "Liberator," the more personal names for God as "Mother," or "Father," "Lover," or "Friend." Whatever it may be, our name for God is our way at any given time of addressing our prayers and beginning the intimate process of confiding our human self to the divine, of giving our otherness over.

Two dangers threaten this simple trust. The first is repression. We keep from our awareness all our primary words for God, those words that leap out of us when we are terror-stricken in accident or illness or facing violence. Fearing that those first names are simply the childish stuff we should have outgrown, we deny their very existence. They still live in us, however, but unadmitted, and usually return to our behavior and feeling by other routes. For example, in trying to teach our children about God as a loving power, we may unwittingly convey a sense of God as a being of whom we should be wary. Urging trust, we may communicate mistrust, because we ourselves have never made room for our own distrust. Denying the existence of these admittedly and appropriately childish gropings toward the unknown, we remain fixed in them because we have allowed them no room to grow or to be influenced by our growing up, by the increased control we have taken in our lives, by our education, by other people and their ideas.

The second danger is idolatry. We admit these images into awareness but then take them to reflect the full concrete reality of God and refuse to move from them. We insist on our own experience to the point of tyranny. We hold onto our image of God in the face of God, choosing our own way over everything. God will be God as we make God to be! We shut ourselves off from God and tyrannize over other people, trying to coerce them to see God as we do. We become bullies, holy terrors.

In idolatry we take the images we have of God as real in themselves instead of real *images*. [12] It is as if we were to take a landscape painting as the countryside itself. It is as if we were just repeating the same words over and over again without really listening to them and through them to what they were actually saying and what responses were being made to them. We paste a label on the surface of ourselves, then willfully forget both the inside self and the outside other.

The alternative to such running way from our deepest selves is to accept our images of God as *real* images that inhabit us, images to which we must join our conscious voice. We must bring all our names for God into our praying. We must even bring our questions and dismissals and self-reproaches. Is this illusion? Is this merely subjective nattering? Are the images really only one-way fantasies, speaking to us about us, or are they in fact two-way exchanges, forming a path *to* God and *from* God?

When accepted as images, these pictures of God may become ladders of ascent and descent, as in Jacob's vision, where we meet God meeting us. [13] God created us as image-making creatures. We assimilate reality as we go along, bit by bit, taking in parts of the world and putting out parts of ourselves. These psychic processes of introjection and projection are to the psyche what breathing is to the body. Karl Barth says even our images for God are reflections of God's reality, as if our images were

God's projections instead of the other way around. In fact, God does match our image-making with a parallel creation, presenting himself in images — as servant, for example, the all-powerful one emptying himself to come to us in a form we can tolerate, that will not overwhelm us, approaching us in a way that will not offend us and make us flee.

Kierkegaard's stories are attempts to build a bridge from our side to God's. In one of them, God is a great emperor who loves a poor maiden. The emperor worries and worries about how to approach the maiden so that she will not run away in fear and not think she is being mocked but can accept that she is loved.[14] The emperor-God accommodates his greatness to our smallness. God creates an image of himself in human proportions in Jesus Christ. If we look at that image with enough confidence in our human processes and the willingness to live and grow with our projections from our childhood totems onward, we will find a connection to the divine Christ contained in the human projections of Jesus.

God answers our images by making visible what Ruysbroeck called the darkness and uncertain way of the divine ground. He makes accessible to us in the language and images of primary speech the depths into which all being sinks.[15] We can face, if we will, the unconditioned and dark uncertainty that swallows every activity into itself, that extraordinary level of being where everything is melted down into the divine and then reflected back to us in the mirror of truth. That mirror is the brightness of the human Jesus in which God beholds himself and in which we behold God. Our images for God and our names for God are met by the images God offers of himself. What gives the major image — Jesus — such persuasion is the fact that in it God becomes a real human person in history, a person who speaks to us by using images.[16]

In the meeting of these two sources of imagery, the human and the divine, we experience our purgation — that sorting, breaking, abandoning and transforming of images in which we are led to confront being itself and are made pliable enough to receive that being into ourselves. Finally, as Scripture and tradition and the experience of those who have used prayer most successfully tell us, we are to be made over into the image of God. We are not to be transformed in an abstract prefabricated way; we are not to be turned into an idea, a disembodied principle, a vagueness of thought to be merged with a generality of feeling. Each of us, with our own particular clusters of images, wishes, needs, and names for God, is to know the transforming work of the Spirit operating within us in the flesh, whether in the world of earth or the universe of ultimate being.

The issue of projection and prayer finds its resolution this way. We must bring all our pictures of God right into our prayers as the centerpiece of our offerings and as something we present to and talk over with God. Those images and names that entrap us will be loosened. Those that block conversation will be winnowed out. Those that push endlessly to center stage, eclipsing both ourselves and the God we address, will be broken. Projections, when we carry them consciously, intelligibly, and trustingly into our prayers bring our primary selves right up to God's presence. We can entrust them because we trust them.

Chapter Four
FANTASY
and PRAYER

Fantasies invade our prayers as they do the rest of our lives. They drift into prayer in the classical form of "Wouldn't it be nice?" or "Wouldn't it be terrible?" As we try to concentrate on praying, they start with the remembrance of a chore to be done or a pleasure to be enjoyed. Before we know it, a whole dinner has been mentally cooked, a room cleaned, a book read, and our prayer is nowhere to be found. Fantasies come to us as daydreams that spin a plot or conjure a drama, often a recurrent one in which we play the central role. Fantasies may rise up from images left over from omnipresent dreams — an insistent questioner of our motives, perhaps, or a figure who aroused strong sexual response. They do not require an invitation.

Old-fashioned prayer manuals caution strongly against the invasion of fantasies.[1] Their authors counsel us to exclude them and even suggest exercises of suppression. The images of fantasy, whether voluntary or involuntary, are distractions from prayer which must be shunned. Modern authors point out, in more contemporary language, the danger of confusing the processes of free-association — that aimless receptive mental state that registers whatever comes to mind — with the more focused work of prayer. We must not mistake self-preoccupation, a sort of narcissistic rumination, for the communings of prayer. Nor should we think we will be protected from this mistake by joining our efforts with others in liturgical prayer. Communal woolgatherings are no less ego-

centric than our private nursings. As groups we possess favorite axes to
grind, political or ethical maxims smuggled into public prayers that
hector their hearers, in effect, to forsake prayer for action.[2]

We can, of course, settle into a set form of praying, a chain of fixed
phrases and sequences that becomes so mechanical we fall into what
Thomas Merton calls a "smug unconscious complacency," where no
truth can break in to free us.[3] We feel no urgent need of God; mental
prayer has degenerated into daydreaming. Real need, nurtured by real
prayer, opens us to God by making unavoidable the shocking fact of how
utterly dependent we are upon his love and his mercy. If we are aware
of our need, we cannot escape our sense of our total poverty of being.
Life is given us. Death will take us. We own nothing.

The critics of fantasy in prayer tend to think that our fantasies distract
us from any awareness of our need and our poverty. Fantasies act as a
deluding smoke screen in which we indulge self instead of listening and
responding to God. We take a very different view of fantasy. If admitted
to full awareness and not made to replace reality or taken as the only
reality, but rather received as one part of reality, we suggest that fantasy
becomes an enlarging means of exposure to being. The task is not to get
rid of fantasy, which usually results in just making ourselves unconscious
of the fantasies that continue anyway below the threshold of awareness.
The task is to know our fantasies and disidentify ourselves from them.

Fantasy opens us to parts of ourselves and our intuitions about life
around us that we usually ignore and that the world deliberately turns
from. Taking note, for example, of our tendency to pray for the sake of
what we can get out of it — solace, health, riches, acclaim, victory for
our side — brings us face-to-face with our pretensions, our self-
aggrandizement, our least useful aggressions and appetites. Fantasy exposes our false self. It also confronts us with our escape hatches, as we
see how we put daily chores and the mere possibility of self-gratification
before what matters, really becoming present to those around us. We see
— if we permit ourselves to see — how we rationalize our own laziness
or stupidity or unwillingness to learn with unacknowledged expectations
that some magic figure will somehow bestow on us as a gift what can
only be learned or gathered from hard experience.

Fantasy brings what lives in the shadows out into the open. Sometimes what emerges is a better self that we have tried to avoid, a genuine

capacity that we have neglected, a wish to give ourselves to something of value that we have blocked with anxieties about failure or financial or emotional security. In fantasy we can see ourselves lingering on thresholds, never coming in fully to be seen, to be used, to be held together at the center of our being.

When looked at knowingly, courageously, and honestly, fantasy ceases to be distracting. Instead, it shows us our distractions. We see how many ways the world gives us to veer off from what matters centrally. The busyness, the competitive pace, the anxieties about having enough, the vanities about others' approval or disapproval of our dress or our ideas or our lifestyle, the constant stress of getting and spending, the false way of achieving a self by triumphing over our neighbor's self — all these worldly pressures can stand out boldly when we pay prayerful attention to our fantasies. Rather than taking us away from the Lord of our being, fantasies thus noticed expose us to the topography of our being. We come to see our ways of struggling toward the light and of dodging it, our wishes to come to the Lord and our escape routes from his summons. Fantasy, when really needed, can sharpen our attention to all the parts of our physical body and our psychic body, all the regions of personality, every part of the corporate body of our working environment, of our family and our faith group and our society. All these different parts war with each other. Each needs to be seen and heard for itself and to find its place in the fascinating complex whole. Noticing our fantasies does not close us off but ushers us, with heightened attention, into this larger world.

This sharpening of awareness is especially important in the areas of our blind spots, those segments of fantasy that touch on elusive dream images, unfocused and less than conscious pictures that we need carefully to bring into consciousness to see and understand.[4] They depict in their blurred way what usually we do not see or want to see — our unintended and thoughtless cruelties to others, our wrong premises that lead us inexorably to wrong conclusions, the certainty that we feel that we are always the victim, that our needs must come first rather than last, that the right outcome always depends on us and no one else, and so on. Our blind areas are those that are concerned with what needs healing and what needs a chance to grow and to be lived. Sentimental faith is exposed in a revealing fantasy as bogus, not tough enough to survive or deserve to survive. Pockets of craziness in our fabric are exposed, showing us where we distort what others say and how we twist their logic. Oversensitivity to being hurt turns up. This is not caused by our delicate nature but by the refusal to use our aggression, forcing it then to turn against us as it inflates the slightest criticism into an all-out attack that levels us. We endow others with our own unlived aggression.

Fantasies received in prayerful attention expose to us the radical pervasiveness of that inner failure that traditional religious language calls "sin." We see it in ourselves, in others we know and love and work with, in the world. Depth psychologists talk about the forces of envy, anger, greed, and hatred alive in us from birth.[5] The person who gives his or her inmost self to prayer is exposed to awareness of those forces head on. The fantasies that take shape around envy, anger, greed, and hatred present us with a sharply personal experience of them in the inescapable details of our lives. For example, when praying we may find ourselves suddenly besieged with anger at someone close to us. We remember the thoughtless action of the other that hurt our feelings. We remember a sarcastic remark made at the expense of our self-esteem. Our mind floods with answers to both the actions and the words. Before we know it, we are carried away into an orgy of outrage and denunciation. A painful little incident has been swelled into the huge proportions of major suffering by remembrance of other occasions when we have been hurt. A rush of anger hurtles through us. It reaches the borders of hate. We feel overcome then by murderous emotions, no longer so clearly caused by another's action. We just want to hurt that other, to spoil its fortune and wreck its peace of mind. What a fantasy has invaded our prayer!

For anyone struggling to pray, these forces of hate are gathered into a relationship with God which makes their presentation only more painful. Now, instead of feeling besieged by autonomous forces of envy and hate, bad as they may be, the praying person experiences them as a rupturing of relationship to God and to his or her own deepest self. It is less a generalized "evil" at this point and more a sense of "sin," a horrified awareness of one's own perjury against truth where truth has shown itself in the most personal of terms. Thus such a praying person shudders at having been swept into a counterfeit self to replace a real one, a dead idol having triumphed over the living God. Awareness grows in these circumstances of what Thomas Merton calls the "deep wound, a fissure of sin that strikes down to the very heart of man's being." We taste the "sickness present in the inmost heart of man estranged from his God by guilt, suspicion and covert hatred."[6]

We must not fight our fantasies when praying, no matter how galling or distracting, for fantasy is an intrinsic part of human life from our earliest months to death. Like a ring on a tree trunk, it grows with us and forms part of our enduring self. If we try to banish fantasies from prayer, we end up fighting endless brush fires as they dart out of us, made stronger, not weaker, by our attempts to deny them. Then we will be really distracted and be unable to pray at all. We will have removed ourselves from a central piece of our groundedness. We will have lost touch with those parts of ourselves and our world that we must experience subliminally and which speak without words. We will have cut ourselves off from one of the most important areas of primary speech.

Perhaps in earlier ages that seem from our perspective to have been all but overwhelmed by the primordial instincts, some measures to suppress fantasy were necessary and effective. They may have had to build secure ego boundaries as a refuge against the swamping tides of the unconscious. But the problem of our age is just the opposite. We are much too secure here and at the same time hopelessly parched, cut off, and ungrounded. We need to grow down into our roots. The Lord of being is down as well as up, out as well as in. All the members of the body need to be collected and brought into prayer. There is no love — of self, of God, of anyone — in cutting off life artificially.

Fantasy is one language through which we can bring our being into our efforts to pray. Art is helpful here. Images from painting, poetry, sculpture, and architecture can awaken dulled, even dead parts of ourselves and stir them to life.[7] There is resurrection, nothing less, in the right sound or movement.

The rhythm of our being is pressed into life, like a trip-hammer mechanism responding to the right signal, by the art that speaks to us. We are not merely pleased by what we see or hear; something fundamental in our fantasy life is confirmed. If nothing else, we are assured through works of art (and not necessarily great ones, but simply those that address us personally in accents that we understand with a particular sense of gratification) that fantasies have a reasonable and important part to play in our world. That is the richness of the great reachings out to God of the poets. It may be the humble things — a mirror, a pulley — of a George Herbert. It may be the humble people — a young girl, a blacksmith — of a Gerard Manley Hopkins. The fantasies such poets weave around their chosen objects and subjects do not decorate prayers. They *are* prayer, holding all the parts of their world together.[8] In time, we may come to recognize that the arts bring a kind of harmony to the imagination without which the enlightenment to which we direct ourselves in prayer would be all but impossible.

Though few of us are poets, most of us meet images in our praying that seem spontaneously to bring together disparate parts of our lives with a daring simplicity. We see the parts of our feelings or thoughts fall into some order so that a new attitude begins to seem possible to us. We think of an upsetting series of misunderstandings with another person. Their words and ours jumble in our minds as we lay these thoughts open before God. Their feelings, our feelings, our past associations, and our searching for God's will in the jumble all come together. Like so many scattered colors lying about, all these bits and pieces gather into a design that has structure and discloses meaning to us, though we would be hard put to express it in words. These are images of *felt* meaning. And like the wonder and pleasure we feel when we find the long-lost piece of a jigsaw puzzle, we may feel that we have been given the missing piece of forgiveness toward another. A sense of the wholeness of the event appears to us. The arts feed our capacity to recognize such designs in our own interior life.

We understand whatever we do of being and creation through metaphor. We should not be able to face the intensity and grandeur of all that is without the mediation of a Mozart piano concerto, for example, or a Dürer portrait, or a perfectly proportioned Renaissance building. Without the many planes of the imagination revealed in such works, we should be reduced to a single-level communication which is simply not capable of grasping the reality around us, much less the world that is beyond our senses.[9] With the intervention of art, reality comes to us on at least two levels, the one on the surface — the figures in the play or on the canvas, the shape of the building, the sound of the music — and the one below, where we discover what it means to us. It does not matter whether we have a full sense of what a baroque composer intended if we are moved to a larger understanding of continuity and wholeness through the long melodic lines and contrapuntual structures of a Bach or a Handel. We are constantly sensitized to our own inner multiplicities by the ironic discourses of an Erasmus, a Joyce, or a Cervantes. We look at plump women with new understanding because of Rubens, at thin men with more appreciation because of Giacometti. If we look long enough and meditate with sufficient intensity on the harmony of art that Kant calls "purposiveness without purpose," we see how fitting it is that Matisse should have left open and unfilled the face of Saint Dominic and without human detail the Stations of the Cross in his "Chapel of the Rosary at Vence." We understand why Mark Rothko should have spent nine months working out the right textures for his black-on-black triptychs at the Houston Chapel, strokings of darkness with which somehow to convey the ineffable.[10] The words of Lao-tze in "The Countenance of the Great Achievement" suggest what the intuitions made tangible in art contribute to our understanding. Where he says "Tao," we might say "being" or "the divine" or "God." We mean what he means. We find the same truth in this kind of art.

> The countenance of the Great Achievement
>   is simply a manifestation of *Tao*.
> That which is called *Tao*
>   is indistinct and ineffable.
> Ineffable and indistinct,
>   Yet therein are objects.
> Deep-seated and unseen
>   Therein are essences.
> The essence is quite real,
> Therein is the vivid truth.
> From ancient times until the present. . . .[11]

In prayer we are constantly driven to use metaphor, especially after the initial noise of talking to God has given way to silence. Prayer, like art and fed by the arts, operates on two levels — surface words and feelings with body responses and postures, and the underlying meaning of prayer for us. In praying we experience the other drawing near, reaching into us. Even when we say these words we are using metaphor, speaking of God's receiving arms, of God's perceiving glance, of God's burning touch. Our most effective metaphors in prayer are effective because through them we can feel the meaning and truth of prayer and the reality of what we pray to. It is in our fantasies that the resources for our most effective metaphors are to be found.

Everything depends on the attitude with which we take account of our fantasies, an attitude that is stripped of its illusions and softened and made pliable by the Spirit of God in prayer. It may be one of the Spirit's major works to open us to the different parts of ourselves and our world through the fantasies that come to light in prayer.[12] As the Bible tells us over and over again, God does not want human sacrifice but relationship and abundant life. God wanted Abraham's first allegiance. He wanted assurance of Abraham's central fidelity, not the death of Isaac. To kill our fantasy or to wound it is not the work of prayer. It may be that the Spirit itself creates "distractions." The Spirit stirs up prayer with fantasy, awakens images and motifs as if getting everything ready to be brought to itself in prayer.

That is the point on which the whole turns — to bring the fantasy to God instead of putting it in place of God, instead of so living the fantasy that we lose both self and God. Here with the aid of fantasy we enter the purgation of prayer. Here we begin the stripping of images, the loss of particular ways to God, the cessation of dependence upon pictures. We are willing now to be left in the dark, to remain in the desert and all the empty places of our heart. Any image that we identify with in place of God or as equal with God's being will be taken from us. It will be dissolved, undone, exposed as wish or fear, too weak to hold. Such images and identifications fall away. If we come into prayer (and at some level we all do begin this way), so caught up in our images of God and images of self in relation to God that we are one with those images, eventually they must be stripped away. That, too, is the work of the Spirit, first to stir up our fantasy images so that we can bring all of our selves and worlds to God, and then to separate us from them, not to obliterate the fantasies, but to make us differentiate ourselves from them.[13]

The process of purgation in prayer is like the process of dis-identification in the life of the psyche. We see a sexual fantasy and experience it, but we are not carried away into it. We feel again a painful childhood loss, but we are not lost to it or in it; we do not depart from our present existence. We may carry in our awareness a strong urge to achieve an end — to make the biggest sale, to write the perfect book, to make the house spotless once and for all. But we are not swept away in the strong currents of our ambition. We allow the fantasies instead of repressing them. But we do not define our being in terms of the fantasies. While they no longer possess us, we do not throw them out and then suffer the fate of that overzealous spiritual housekeeper of the parable who threw out one devil and returned only to find seven devils. We have them and do not have them. We contain them instead of being contained by them. That is hard, painful work, necessary work, rewarding work.[14]

Prayer is one of the most effective ways to do this work. For when we pray for our enemy, for example, we feel again all the hurt and anger and anguish gathered around that person. Yet we pray that God's good will may operate in the situation, and in that person. And so we feel our anguish and yet are separated from it. We cannot wallow in it or get stuck there. But painfully, we can struggle to hold to God's merciful presence even in the midst of our vengeful urges. In the middle of a sexual fantasy we may offer its bursting energy into God's hands, to be used for God's will, thus still feeling it but no longer controlling its outcome. We confide it and entrust it to God's guidance, to be used or to be laid aside, as we shall sometime see and be shown and understand. In the midst of moving toward death we may register the deep fear of pain and of the unknown and call down God's presence into it, right there with us. Nothing is to separate us from the love of God, or the Spirit, in Christ, not life or death or even our best pictures of God, not even our finest hopes for relationship with the divine.

Temptation comes most strongly not in the most obvious evils but in the subtlest. Those values that are our best are the ones that threaten our prayer life and thus our hold on the divine. Even that spontaneous life that the Spirit stirs up in us, often more colorful and promising than the life we live, must not be put before God.[15] We must bring it to God in our prayers and let God bring us forward by this stripping action. That is how we are brought in prayer to disidentify with these parts of ourselves and to put in their place the values of our world which are frequently some of the best parts of our world. While their place is a good one, it is neither our place nor the Lord's. The values are means, not ends. God is the end, where we meet not refractions nor reflections of being but being itself.

Chapter Five
LIVING
with FANTASY

Fantasy fully accepted in prayer becomes a rhythmic movement in one's life that may lead to a meeting with being. Here music can offer guidance and direction to the praying person. The alterations of sound and silence that we meet in music, of dynamic variations ranging from fortissimo to pianissimo, of every kind of beat and pulse, can evoke and support the rhythms of primary speech. We burst out toward being with a heart full of images and desires, crowded with rich fragments of ourselves. We fall utterly silent, lost in the timeless moment, still as an emptied pot is still. We are seized by a fantasy, and then stripped of it. But the images return, sometimes new ones, sometimes the old ones in changed form. The spirit works us like bread dough, leavening the lump of our inertia with images that make us rise, expand, and grow light in weight. Then it punches us down and the fantasies escape from us like so much hot air. We are pummeled and molded to fit a shape that takes its origin outside ourselves — the image of the being in which we were created. We are made to conform to its dimensions, firmer and larger than any we could fashion by ourselves. Then we can rise again to our full height. Prayer is a growing process.

A major step in the world of primary speech is learning how to have our fantasies and stand aside from them simultaneously. This apparently contradictory stance is intrinsic in all subsequent movements of the spiritual life. In its simultaneous gathering in and giving up, it rehearses us for the paradoxes and antinomies of the life of the spirit, where affirmation comes in denial and withdrawal may be the only way to move ahead. We are like a dancer who learns certain basic movements, repeats them, depends on them, builds on them in the most complicated and advanced executions of the body, and then can forget all about them, not losing them but dropping them from full consciousness when a new world of movement must be entered.[1] In the same way, we receive and hold in awareness the most fullbodied fantasies for the longest time, building on them, never pushing them away. And yet we are able, when the time comes, to relinquish them, to let them disappear from consciousness altogether.[2] The spirit finds us this way and firms us. We grow into a capacity for graceful flexibility and for the endless ups and downs of prayer, not only pliable in this life that bounds between extremes but also durable.

What does this mean in practice? It means we take our fantasies seriously. It means we offer them to God. We have them and we don't have them. We are rich and poor, hungry and satisfied, full and empty simultaneously. Our most fearsome fantasies remain with us — we are murderer and victim, sick unto death and healer of the dying, victor and defeated. We extend across worlds into every condition of men and women and are connected with them, as ourselves, in our living persons. We become bigger, more stretched out, more transparent, less densely compacted around our tight little identity. Our fantasies become lenses through which we see God's spirit working at us, on us, and in us. We see through our fantasies and are less apt now to be duped by them.[3]

In our increased size, in our greater transparency, our identities become more vivid and secure. Sharply, strongly they are our own. They belong to us, but not as a lifeless piece of property, and so we can receive them as we could not before. Because we can stand aside from our fantasies, we are freer. An element of play enters our prayers. We find in the words and images of primary speech a sense of humor. We come close enough in our lightness of spirit to see and enjoy the playful aspect of the divine. We laugh in our prayer. God must long for a funny story, we think, instead of still another lugubrious hymn or turgid meditation, still another solemn promise, still another tortured, pompous confession in which even our sins are matters of pride. One of the most lethal perversions of religion is to present it as so constantly dreary, so dull and joyless. What, after all, is the purpose of the life of the spirit — to show ourselves off as small, mean, and boastful, or to glorify God? "The glorification of God," Jürgen Moltmann reminds us, "lies in the demonstrative joy of existence."[4] Do we enjoy talking to God? Do we cry out when all our images abandon us? Do we laugh when they return in changed form, free now to be with us, light, graceful, even funny, no longer unremittingly grim, no longer demanding compulsive responses? Any prayer that bores us must surely tax even an infinite patience.

Consenting to the stirring up and stripping down of the spirit enlarges the space of our prayers. Its great mark is this new playfulness. We can make active use of the fantasies that come to us, like a child's building blocks. We construct a fabulous tower and knock it down again, inspect an image, thick with color and filled with a gathering of lines, a palace of the imagination unique in itself. We wonder about its intricacies the way a child wonders about the construction of a flower suddenly stumbled on in a field. And then we see that it is withering away, and we find the withering no less fascinating than the initial appearance of this prodigy of being. We experiment with different ways of praying, different ways of coming to it and living with it, knowing now more clearly than before that there is no one way, no set method, and there cannot be.[5] We learn to respond in the moment to the moment in which abiding eternal being appears to us.

One of the experiments that can only deepen our conversation in prayer parallels a discovery made in looking at our projections onto the divine. There we discovered the name or names we had for God. Here, both having and holding onto our fantasies and standing aside from them, we discover how we name our self in relation to God. After much experience in prayer, we may even come to know God's name for us. At this beginning level we see how we see ourselves in relation to God, with what voices the primary speech of our prayers presents us to God and to ourselves. Jacob Boehme, for example, confesses that he is nothing but "a swineherd," "a perjurer," and beseeches God to "smash" his "heart and soul." Brother Lawrence pictures himself as a piece of stone out of which God, like a mason, will make a statue. In his prayers, he asks God to make His image perfect in his soul. At other times he sees himself as if uplifted without any effort on his part, but suspended and "held in God as in a centre and place of rest."[6] Jacob Boehme, in his alchemy of the mystical life, sees our "true life" as "a choked fire; in some even as the fire shut up in a stone." We kindle that fire in our prayers, "by right and earnest turning to God," which may even make us "capable of the divine fire."[7]

The way we discover what and who we are, as we present ourselves to God, comes when we discover the main threads that run through our fantasies. We see through the language and images of fantasy that questioning of God, that demand, that hope, that fear, that need around which our life has revolved. This, too, is a way of naming ourselves, on the basis of which we address God. This central questioning of God is one of the ways we reach most directly to God.[8] It is a road on which to move to the divine and a place in which to rest in the divine. It is the basis on which we approach God.

Is our central question, for example, whether or not God exists?[9] Do we ask how we should live if God does exist? Is our central question: What is it that makes so many of us turn away from our best selves? Is it: How can we entrust to God's providence those we love most dearly? Is it the terror and confusion of suffering: How can there be such pain and misery in a universe of goodness, how such injustice, such a multiplicity of evils? Whatever the question, it is there we will meet our crucifixion and resurrection. There we are identified. There we will be forced to let go. There we will be tried and brought through the many deaths of disidentifying to a life in many ways altogether new to us.[10] That new life comes from the discovery that when we have entrusted to God what we hold most dear or most frightening, we gain one entirely made over, made for us and our own true self.

This gift to the self benefits not only ourselves but the world around us. We all owe a great deal to individuals who try to go on praying despite the feeling that they are simply wandering in the dark, despite the confusing contradiction of a constant loss of images and arrival of new images. What they are doing is constantly plowing up the ground of our collective unconscious life and preparing us all for the richness of a new spiritual life, as earlier they may have afflicted us all with their emptiness and desolation. They make the ground we share fertile for the growth of new symbols, symbols that are not so private that they speak only to a few of us nor so public that they omit the strong accents of each individual's primary speech. Urs von Balthasar points out the social effects of prayer: "Contemplatives are like great subterranean rivers, which, on occasion, break out into springs at unexpected points, or reveal their presence only by the plants they feed from below."[11] We are watered by these sudden eruptions from the contemplative underground. We are fed with a symbolic richness we had never expected, even though our fantasies more than hinted at it. On this fine food our spiritual imagination grows fat.

We build up in prayer the capacity for symbols of the divine that take us step by step into God's mystery.[12] We often feel abandoned there, as if we have left a safe diving board, stepping from it to plunge into unseen waters far below us. This having sure footing and losing it ushers us into the mystery of the survival of our lost images. Only when we despair of reaching God can we see that God is always reaching to us. The images and the fantasies are both essential and irrelevant. What emerges as the sure path is the reality which the images simultaneously reveal and obscure. In the long view, the periods of darkness and aridity can be seen as essential to the path, just as vital to our progress and understanding as the moments of light and fulfillment. They are not to be regretted but rather to be embraced.

It is only too easy to misinterpret the saints in their descriptions of years of dryness and darkness and unnecessarily discourage ourselves in our own efforts to pray, fearing that all of this will be too much suffering to endure. It may be that the saints speak of arid periods from a later perspective, from visions of completeness, purpose, and clarity that set all that happened previously in a more shadowy and threatening light.[13]

At each stage of prayer God gives us what we need. It really is true — the dark is light enough. We must follow here with our fantasies that central principle of Francis de Sales: "Ask for nothing and refuse nothing."[14] We find, then, in retrospect that what began as the free association of conflicting fantasies was actually pulling all its parts, all *our* parts, toward a central focusing on God's being. If sustained and accepted when necessary and let go of when necessary, these fantasies can lead us to the achievement of a contemplation that can effortlessly look at the real.

Chapter Six
FEAR
and PRAYER

Fear can pull us right down into the center of ourselves. Fear can make us sweat or turn clammy cold. Fear can upset the stomach and make the heart race. Fear is itself frightening. It is all the more frightening when not really acknowledged and prepared for. The most devastating effect of fear is our fear of it. Prayer makes a place for fear and prayer puts fear in its place.

Praying brings us soon enough to our fears. The fear that arrives early on in prayer is fear of silence. Prayer introduces silence into the turmoil of our daily life.[1] Trying to sit still or lie still and to get still within ourselves exposes us to the noise we live in almost constantly, as if an inner radio or phonograph were playing continuously. Sometimes we can pretend that the clamor does not exist, but not in prayer. Prayer makes us hear all our noise. At first it may be refreshing. We can take notice of the noise and get some distance from it. Then we really listen to each of the voices speaking and pay attention to what they are saying. Primary speech is imperious to the praying soul. It commands attention to the wishes, the hopes, the fears, all the bits of ourselves that it brings to us. We must listen, and that is good. Such listening sets inner things in order and gives us as a result some freedom.

We begin to listen for the lordly voice that is not ours as our own many little voices begin to collect themselves and come to be recollected in this typical first stage of prayer. But then silence enters, and we grow afraid that no other voice is there, no lordly presence. We become fearful, believing that no answer will come. All our prayerful "insights" seem merely secret efforts of our own. They are not objectively true, really there. Worse yet, as we go on praying, our beneficent, faithful images and fantasies may dry up or cease altogether. So even our own calming voice, which could compensate us for lacks or hurts or particularly anguishing problems, can no longer be heard.

Soon we fear we have nothing to say or do that can move us to God in our prayers. Nothing sustains itself. Images fade and fall away. Fantasies grow thin. We cannot concentrate on meditative reading, in Scripture or prayer book or anything else. We wake in the middle of the night besieged by our fears and feel utterly abandoned to them.[2] There is no counseling word, no heartening vision, no calming insight or plan of action. We are not our own creatures; we are pushed this way and that by the most elementary fears, and worse, we feel embarrassed to be so frightened by the things that frighten us. In our fearful state, we worry that people do not like us and that they will not want to see us. We worry about what others will think of what we say or will think when we do not say anything at all. We fear their anger, neglect, and judgment. We fear we lack the heart to produce any fresh feeling or the intelligence to create a new idea. We fear our work does not really amount to anything important and never has. We fear we will not have any work or will do what we have to do so badly that we will lose our job and not get another one. We fear we will never marry or be found desirable as a friend or lover. We fear we will lose the mate we have. We tremble when we think of the shallowness of our relationships. We fear we will not be accepted by those who have authority over us and will be declared a failure and banished. We fear isolation, unceasing vulnerability, impotence. We fear physical pain, aging, dying. We fear the force of our own distress or depression. We fear being so easily bogged down, bringing no identifiable goodness into the world.

Praying takes us right into the middle of these fears and opens their constant little trickle into a swift running stream, for in prayer every early effort to still our fears only intensifies them. We try all the familiar tricks — reciting familiar set phrases, psalms, hymns. We count numbers, we do breathing exercises. But fear persists and will not be removed by any of the consecrated relaxation procedures, by tranquilizers, by liquor, or drugs. Like the collective effort of a congress of mice in our walls, fear gnaws at us, weakening and threatening to bring down our house.

We call out to God. But nothing comes back. Bereft even of the wishes, fantasies, and images that once took us toward the divine and helped us see how close by God already was, we feel impossibly alone and helpless. Images that bridged our distance from God now are too far away from us, distant and useless. All our false gods lie exposed like so many discarded Christmas wrappings. But even there, in that debris, we cannot find a shred of the presence of God. Instead, emptiness and silence now menace us. Stripped of all the ways we once would have used to come to God, to seek being, disidentified from all our idols, we are close to despair.

This is where prayer makes a place for fear. At the bottom of our hopes, dismal in spirit, frightened by the great gulf of silence which seems to surround us, we discover the powers of reflection. We begin to discriminate among the noises that earlier beset us so strongly. Is it fear of incompetence at work, unattractiveness to others in social life, the inability to love or to be loved? Which one of these zones of fear is really ours? Or is it none of them? Or all of them? There is an extraordinary literature of fear to help us answer these questions and deal with them.

Is our fear, for example, simply the kind of "prolonged, irresistible dissatisfaction" about which Franz Kafka writes? In his diaries, Kafka shows how this kind of unhappiness with oneself can move step by step, from a cacophony of nervous chattering voices, to a brooding restlessness in which one cannot work, to a reflective silence. There, at last, still at some distance from his writing program, he puts words together that have the stature of some of the best passages in his novels *The Trial* and *The Castle*. He shows us what this kind of making place for fear through prayer amounts to.

Some years before the composition of either of his great novels, in a 1912 diary entry, Kafka muses on the assaults of his many devils. He recognizes that if he "can do something" then he "can do it without superstitious precautions." That leads him to the use we make in our imagination of the devil.

> If we are possessed by the devil, it cannot be by one, for then we should live, at least here on earth, quietly, as with God, in unity, without contradiction, without reflection, always sure of the man behind us.

His face would not frighten us, for as diabolical beings we would, if somewhat sensitive to the sight, be clever enough to sacrifice a hand in order to keep his face covered with it. If we were possessed by only a single devil, one who had a calm, untroubled view of our whole nature, and freedom to dispose of us at any moment, then that devil would also have enough power to hold us for the length of a human life above the spirit of God in us, and even to swing us to and fro, so that we should never get to see a glimmer of it and therefore should not be troubled from that quarter.

That shrewd piece of reasoning leads him to conclude that the devil we have invented cannot be a single embodiment of evil who brings us our difficulties.

Only a crowd of devils could account for our earthly misfortune. Why don't they exterminate one another until only a single one is left, or why don't they subordinate themselves to one great devil? Either way one would be in accord with the diabolical principle of deceiving us as completely as possible. With unity lacking, of what use is the scrupulous attention all the devils pay us? It simply goes without saying that the falling of a human hair must matter more to the devil than to God, since the devil really loses that hair and God does not.[3]

That kind of reflection is an occasion for comfort. The devil — which is to say, everything inside and outside us that incites us to despair or even lesser discouragement with ourselves — cannot be a singular force, of our own making or anybody else's. No one devil can account for our misery. That should retire our concentration on one particular source of fear. It is not simply that we cannot love or be loved, do well at work or in relations with other people. It is not a general ineffectiveness which has settled with singular intensity upon us. We can dismiss any such single claim on our spirits, for that is not the way our personal devils get at us.

Dostoevsky dramatized the affliction in that brilliant prognosis and diagnosis of the nature of the modern world, *The Devils*. We are possessed, as he showed, by a whole carload of little devils. We need, like the devil-invaded man cured by Jesus, to have them chased into a herd as large as that of the Gadarene swine. We "still do not arrive at any state of well-being," Kafka concludes, "so long as the many devils are within us."[4]

What we must capture — or recapture — from the silence of med-

itation is the confidence that Kafka expresses so well in the instance of
"the falling of a human hair." We may be tempted to call this a metaphor
and let it go at that. It is simply a way, we may think, of indicating the
difference between the devil's inadequacies and the Lord's omnipotence.
Conventional thoughts, we may say; no more. Yet it is a literal truth to
those who understand the distinction, and a magnificent one. The devil
must rush around (or rather all the devils must), hoping to gather what
few hairs can be found. The Lord, on the other hand, is a keeper of all
things, things of the flesh as well as things of the spirit. God does not lose
anything. That is why Gerard Manley Hopkins tells us to give it all over
to God's keeping, and to give it now, to give everything, not only the big
but the little, not only the miseries but the delights, the glory, the beauty:

> deliver it, early now, long before death
> Give beauty back, beauty, beauty, beauty, beauty, back to
> God, beauty's self and beauty's giver.
> See; not a hair is, not an eyelash, not the least lash lost;
> every hair
> Is, hair of the head, numbered.

Hopkins speaks right to our concern for our failures, our worry about
our inadequacies of all kinds, our plentiful fears. Why should we worry
so when everything we have, everything we do or fail to do, everything
we achieve or fail to achieve, is held onto and understood and cared for:

> O then, weary then why should we tread? O why are we so haggard
> at the heart, so care-coiled, care-killed, so fagged, so fashed,
> so cogged, so cumbered,
> When the thing we freely forfeit is kept with fonder a care,
> Fonder a care kept than we could have kept it. . . .

Where is it kept?

> Where kept? Do but tell us where kept, where. —
> Yonder. — What high as that! We follow, now we follow. — Yonder,
> yes yonder, yonder,
> Yonder.[5]

It is not an easy confidence for most of us to manage. It takes the
assaults of our many little devils, the engulfing silence, and the meditations that rise to prayer in that silence to lead us, somewhat uneasily,
still frightened perhaps, to "give beauty back." It takes as much

to give over misery, too — and not to demand the tangible assurance of a written contract with our Lord, or a trip to the storehouse where the fallen hairs are kept. Kafka, writing out of his difficulties, "in a state of some confusion," to his fiancee Felice Bauer, makes the same point:

> Are you aware, and this is the most important thing, of a continuous relationship between yourself and a reassuringly distant, if possibly infinite height or depth? He who feels this continuously has no need to roam about like a lost dog, mutely gazing around with imploring eyes; he never need yearn to slip into a grave as if it were a warm sleeping bag and life a cold winter night; and when climbing down the stairs to his office he never need imagine that he is careening down the well of the staircase, flickering in the uncertain light, twisting from the speed of his fall, shaking his head with impatience.[6]

Even if we come to accept Hopkins' God-as-Keeper-of-Fallen-Hairs or Kafka's Reassuringly-Distant-Height-or-Depth, we will not be assured of perfect serenity and constant ease. While neither Hopkins nor Kafka ever found such respite from fear and uncertainty, they found something better. They discovered the resources with which to write their extraordinary parables of fear and of the assuagement of fear in faith. It is a troubled faith they offer us, consistent with their problematical being and ours. Kafka's God dwells at the distance of *The Castle,* perched high over us, always, as Hopkins puts it, yonder, yonder, yonder. But we need not and must not always accuse ourselves, as Joseph K. does in *The Trial,* and assure ourselves only of sacrificing ourselves to the mean devils we have allowed to possess us in our incessant self-harrassment. We can bring ourselves into the place that prayer makes for our fears and find ourselves there, willing to face ourselves, in the eloquent silence of prayer.[7]

And there we must be — sitting, kneeling, walking, silent. We grow acutely ashamed of the many ways we have found to manufacture God in our own image. We are uncomfortable to discover how mixed up our efforts to pray have become — the way we seek to wheedle privileges, to get favors, to seem to deserve them, to fall back into a womb-like safety, to evade responsibility, to avoid finding and holding onto our own authority, to run away from the world.

The silence that prayer unveils may chasten us. Abandoned by our little gods, and seemingly delivered to our many devils, the old-fashioned religious vow of chastity takes on new meaning for us now. Chastity here means being stripped of competing claims, made ready to center on the one great claim — being disidentified from our many incomplete loves so we can give our self to the one fulfilling love. Everything now goes in one direction. We hand over our fears of others' disapproval to God. Equally, we offer up our wish for others' approval. We present all our little gods to God. Purity, says Kierkegaard, is to will one thing.[8] The silence of prayer orders all the lesser things to go through a door opening to the one thing, the primary voice of God.

That voice moves along what Max Picard calls "the wall of silence." Silence, Picard makes clear, signifies more than words. Silence is the primary speech in which God and humanity speak to each other:

> God became man for the sake of man. . . . A layer of silence lies between this event and man, and in this silence man approaches the silence that surrounds God himself. . . .
>
> It is a sign of the love of God that a mystery is always separated from man by a layer of silence. And that is a reminder that man should also keep a silence in which to approach the mystery.

Unlike our silence, God's silence is not different from his speech; "word and silence are one in God." God's is "a self-giving silence," pouring into us.[9] Thus the silence we so fear in prayer comes to be a principal part of praying. Silence makes us chaste. Silence makes us articulate. In it God reaches into us to gather all our rackety voices into the calm that issues from differentiating from everything else the one important thing — looking toward God.[10]

The more we look to God, the more our fear deepens, at first. We realize how utterly poor we are. The religious vow of poverty takes on new force. We are utterly dependent on what is given us — life itself, the personalities of the parents who gave us birth and raised us, the time in history in which we find ourselves, with its identifying problems and possibilities that shape our cultural identities. We depend on our talents and our limitations, the strengths and the weaknesses in our own characters that we develop or neglect. But nothing finally belongs to us; nothing in us is autonomous. All is held in our relationships with other people and with the mysterious source of being. We must see that whatever we have we have in dialogue, in contingency, in connection with others who are beyond us and beyond our ultimate control. Even what is lovable in us depends on someone else's recognizing it and bringing it out in the open.

When we go beyond the mere sentiment of poverty in religion to an inner conviction of our destitution, our fear is quickly engaged again. We see with utmost clarity that sin is refusal of this poverty. Sin's major way of tempting us is through stupidity of the heart, what Christian doctrine calls "the privation of knowledge." We ignore the evidence of our senses that tells us how much our mood and our will depend on the weather, on what we have eaten and how much sleep we have had. We ignore the evidence of our emotions that tells us how much our good will depends on how others speak to us, how easily we arm ourselves if we feel they look down on us, how quick we are to avenge the offense to our self-esteem when they overlook us. On the other side of this strenuous experience, how easily we expand into our better selves if spoken to kindly, lovingly, with respect! We ignore the evidence of what we know. We forget that what strikes us as original insight comes to us as a gift out of our dialogues with other people, with books, with tradition.[11] We may have worked hard in those dialogues to understand and to discover insights. Work is necessary. But when the new understanding arrives and the insight falls into place, we know we did not create it but simply received it.

In our ignorance we are tempted to choose false crosses over the real ones — false suffering, that hurts but brings no healing, over real suffering, whose pain softens us and changes us radically. From such mistaken choices, say Augustine and Boehme, rises all the unrest in the world.[12] The false cross always tempts us by the promise of riches. We can be in control, fully in charge, we think. We can be the one who directs, who is independent, uncreated, autonomous, not contingent, not a being-who-can-be-only-in-relation-to-others. We are like the parent who suffers with a child who will not grow up, who drains his parents of the resources of patience and good will as well as more tangible supports. But usually it is parents who bind their children and prevent their getting free. Such parents insist on seeing themselves as the only suppliers of what their children need, all the while complaining of their children's dependency and ingratitude. But aggrandizing parents of that kind refuse to set their children free by cutting off their supplies, so that they can find their own sources within themselves and can find their own relation to reality. Such parents' false and unnecessary suffering breeds enmity between themselves and their children and destroys the goodness of both.

True suffering by parents would be to face their failure in fostering in their children a reliable self-esteem, and to feel remorse. True suffering would be to face the fear that their children cannot stand on their own and yet to let them go anyway, for perhaps they amount to much more than the parents think. Perhaps other people will give them the help the parents cannot offer. True suffering here is to renounce control and accept interior poverty — to know and accept the fact that they give their children what they can, of both good and bad, and that they are not in any case the ultimate source of their children's being.[13]

Children, in their first conscious experiences of religion, often understand this, even when their parents do not. They recognize in their curious shuttling back and forth between good and bad behavior something undependable in the moral atmosphere they inhabit. While they do not have full control over their own actions, neither do their parents. This is not simply because children at times feel they must defy every authority, and especially the parental. Children in the pivotal years that reach from just before puberty to just after discover again the ambivalence of values. Unlike the infant who reaches what Melanie Klein calls the "position of reparation," with the recognition that its mother is not all good when the milk flows freely or all bad when the milk stops, this pubescent-in-the-making finds the whole structure of supports for life undependable, wobbly, incomplete.[14] The same situation can produce delight and despair. A parent, a teacher, a beloved friend may hug and kiss and then, seconds later, turn around and bat one over the head. What a mess — great compliments, doting words, then total condemnation and relegation to the outposts of civilization. The whole spectrum of responses is covered, which is bewildering enough. But even more startlingly, it all seems to the child to be occasioned by actions not very different from one another. What is more, as far as the child can see, his or her actions were all decently motivated or even intended in every case to bring pleasure and elicit warm and loving responses.

As children caught in such situations meditate on the monstrous double binds that seem to hold them prisoner, they sometimes begin to grasp nothing less than the complex metaphysics of freedom in which we all live our lives. With a child's grace, they reduce the complex to its simple components. The same situation really can yield good or bad feelings, not only in others but in oneself. What was intended to be a good action can draw a reproof; a bad one, a pat on the head or a kiss. One can face this set of contradictions about oneself and the moral universe with depression, bafflement, or frustration; or one can find in the apparently irreconcilable paradoxes a larger controlling presence. While there is no easy explanation, to those who make sense of these confounding paradoxes this way there is perhaps something better. Desolation becomes hope. Contradiction becomes rapprochement. The interior life begins.

The mid-nineteenth century Russian writer Konstantin Leontiev has a passage in one of his novels that reflects this process of interiorization. His narrator speaks of the moments in childhood religious experience when, in "the sadness of solitude," there was mingled "the fear of being punished beyond the grave, with the hope of finding succour while still among the living." He remembers the joy given him by his aunt's icon and the light shining on it. He also remembers the unhappiness he felt when he left church too early or spilled bits of communion wafer: "I saw myself as one who had abused something innocent and indulgent." Reading the last chapters of the Old Testament stirred in him a "feeling of barely audible, barely noticeable, sweet expectation. . . . The dawn of a better life seemed to be awaiting the whole world. There was no light as yet, and one felt both sad and relieved." The coming and going of Christ elicits a similar response. After Jesus's appearance to the disciples on the way to Emmaus, everything seems deserted. Leontiev describes the child's reaction in words wonderfully reflective of the kind of puzzlement and peace that accompany one's first significant meditation on the possibility of encountering the Lord. Which is it that most consoles us, that most frees us, that most uses and quiets our fears, the presence that leads to departure or the absence that promises return? Christ has been and gone —

> How deserted it all seems! As though after dinner when it is no longer hot, you might enter a large green garden which no one is using and where the shadows cast by the trees grow more and more elongated. As though the person closest to one had departed from the house and the garden, in which he could have strolled had he wished. And something

new was about to begin, was about to glimmer. . . . But what was it?
Even then I could not explain it, nor can I do so now.[15]

God acts like a parent toward us, loving us, endowing us, and at the
same time setting us free to find our own resources and responses. The
poverty we so fear becomes the entrance to our inner riches: we own
nothing, we possess no one, not even our children who display the face
of human dependence so vividly to us. To take this way of poverty wakes
us up to the plenitude that daily is given us. We breathe easily and eat
well, we think, a friend speaks to us, we are loved. We have only to lose
our ease in any one of these things to know their priceless value. The poor
in spirit are indeed filled. All we have is given us, and given (we will see
if we look hard enough) in abundance.

Just at this point of recognition of our abundance, our fear may
intensify to a greater degree than ever before. We find fear for those we
love and for what we value. We fear losing life itself through a painful
illness, a helpless dying of old age, a slow dismissal of being. We fear
even more our child's suffering, in illness, in an accident, in the inevitable clashes with others and with our inner selves in conflict with our outer
worlds. Fear of the assault of despair against self or friends or loved ones
plagues us. We recognize the despair that catapults toward suicide. What
a terror it is that those close to us can break down, can lose their way in
the world, can lose their souls, and we may not be able to help. There
may be no help. War may take over our world once again; whole generations of young people may be maimed, tortured, disillusioned beyond
repair. We see only too easily how many others suffer from hunger,
how many imaginations are starved, how much pain is caused by systematic meanness, greed thrusting for power, destroying our world, wasting
its bounty, spoiling its beauty, making extinct its strange and wonderful creatures.

There are sufferings larger and more inclusive than ones that afflict
us personally. In them, we fear the destruction of values, we tremble to
see even the notion of value become blurred beyond definition, impossible for many to grasp. We fear that we cannot control evil, not in the
world, not in ourselves. The world's "perfect solutions" turn out to be
worse than the problems which occasion them. Not only large-scale
revolutions but also small-scale reforms wreak havoc. Our urge to solve

everything, perhaps to play not God or even his Grand Inquisitor but just his junior minister, all but destroys us. That is how temptation lures us, enticing us to keep choosing, in generation after generation, the fruit of the tree of good and evil. We insist on the apple. Power belongs in our hands. The tree of good and evil always grows out of *our* version of reality, *our* sense of timing, *our* definition of goals, *our* understanding of suffering and its appeasement. With goodhearted grace, concern, and endless strength, we veer right off course.[16]

We have decided that the cross is obsolete. Who needs it? What a tempting choice: *our* version of the good life, of the good death. All that we lose as a result is the encounter with the God who meets us in our fear and uncertainty.

God does not ever altogether remove our fear. What he does is to join us in it. He is there where we are afraid. That is the way of the cross, of the tree of life. That is the way of the God who enters our life even in the face of death. That is the way of the vow of obedience in religion. It strikes to the heart of our fear. It tells us to be obedient to our love even unto death. It instructs us not to run or attempt to run from the inescapable fact of the contingency of our being. We cannot protect those we love from suffering. We cannot be sure that we will hold onto our own sanity. We cannot guarantee peace or good will on earth. There is no sure answer to these great fears. There is only one help for them — to surrender them into God's hands. We must do all we can and still give them over into God's care. Our fear brings us right to the point where we can accept the fact that we are subject to God's will and not simply to our own. We can do much with our will. Best of all, in prayer, we can move it towards God's will.

Change comes at this point, a change that altogether makes over our fear. Far from being afraid that no one will answer, that nothing will be there, we are now fearfully aware that God is near and will answer. Like that prickling of antennae outdoors on a dark night when we sense an animal nearby, we feel another presence in our prayer. Fear opens us to that presence. And then we thank God, even for our fears.

Chapter Seven
PRAYER
and AGGRESSION

Praying opens up our aggression.[1] We discover ambivalent feelings toward God and uncertain notions of God's nature and our own. We want to pray and we do not want to. We think we should pray and we wish we did not have to. We long to pray and we dread it. We think of the God of grace, but then remember the God of wrath. Heaven is promised, but hell threatens, too. God is merciful, but also jealous. In the firm floor of prayer a wide crack has begun, soon to spread into an unbridgeable gap.

Prayer makes it impossible to avoid aggression. We notice how irritable we are, how hard to please, how easily made discontented, jumpy, nervous, quarrelsome. We are full of restless, unchanneled energy, turning back on itself. Gusts of vigorous emotion confront us, ready to be lived, but we do not know where or how. Surges of determination and extreme resolutions burst through in prayer, as if we had suddenly discovered wild horses living in our house, kicking to get out, horses that need to be ridden, guided and enjoyed.

Aggression enters our prayers with the fervor of our pleas for ourselves. We speak of our needs. We cry out our hopes. We excuse ourselves for our defects, our failures, our bedeviling fantasies.[2] If we think ourselves right, we are appalled that others do not see that and say so. If we think ourselves wrong, we are determined not to be judged too harshly, by others or by God, and all the more so if our own self-judgments are harsh.

On the other hand, our aggression may show itself in an opposite way, in diffused form. We do not know what we think or feel. We flop about, unwilling to make decisions. We hope others will do something that will decide an issue for us. We talk our insights or possibilities away, parking them on others instead of working on them ourselves. We show aggressiveness by the way we drift along, half-clear, half-determined, half-decided, until everyone around us is ready to scream at us because of our refusal to coagulate or to act.

Aggression usually scares us in prayer because it threatens separation from God and an almost impossible immersion in self. Aggression announces itself negatively as anger or withdrawal. We close up against God like a fist, defiant, challenging. Or we live our aggression passively, sinking like a lump of inertia into our withdrawal, expecting the other, God, to do all the work of getting in touch.[3] Yet we resist any move in our direction and fill up with reproach and self-pity.

Aggression announces itself positively as a sudden buoyant sense of self. We want to step away from childish images of God and grow beyond our dependency on protective kindness, where God is a watchful mother into whose arms we have crawled. We want to give up our fear of authority, where God is a father whose commands always restrict us and blunt our initiative. Aggressive impulses burst from our prayers, like muscles breaking the seams of our child's clothing. We no longer want a God in the soft colors of infancy — pinks, blues, pale yellows. We want robust colors now — crimson, emerald green, purple, gold. Our aggressive energies lead us to question our old images of God, to break them, and to endure their loss. We go off on our own, looking to fill out our self. We seek a God who affirms a wide, deep, vigorous self, not a stingy disapproving God, not a nagging thundering God, not a confining, too tender God.[4] We want to blast off.

Prayer makes it possible for us to assimilate our aggression. What otherwise might be at the least a mild exercise in self-indulgence, and at worst the kind of naked aggression that brings violence into the world, becomes in prayer a channel for the discovery and exposure of self. But it takes several forms, both negative and positive. And just as it is an enabling force for prayer, prayer is a supporting environment for differentiating aggression.

Aggression in its negative form creates problems in prayer. When we pray we open up to what occupies our minds and hearts. Anger at others and outrage at their stupid behavior can quickly take us over. While trying to pray, we are taken off into reliving what "they" said and what "we" said, wishing they or we had said something else. We replay old scenes and fantasize new and better ones. We fill up with resentment, hurt, rage. It is frightening to feel the intensity of our anger bursting within us like waves of hot lava erupting from our core. Appalled, we feel the rising urge for revenge against our enemies. Sadistic fantasies of what we would like to do to them invade us.[5] We condemn others' thoughtlessness and injustice. We are appalled by their meanness to us and to others. We hold them in contempt.

It is exhausting to feel such negative aggression — and prayer leads us straight to it. To hold this hostility in awareness and not be overwhelmed by it and taken off into its turbulence taxes our energies to the limit. The irony is that we need more aggression to hold our own against capture by aggression. To try to practice Christian forgiveness and charity toward our neighbor and to pray for our enemies seems beyond our strength. We both hate with a hot hate and want to do what Jesus commanded. We want to stand with the truth we know to be true — that violence breeds only violence, that forgiveness and love can bring peace.

Two dangers threaten us at this point. The first, a maneuver that Freud attacked vehemently, is to repress all our angry aggressive feelings and transfer them to God, who will take vengeance against our enemy.[6] Such repression weakens faith. It takes the life out of it, makes it treacly-sweet and smirky-good, and even worse, sentimental on the surface and sadistic underneath. Such a faith is not tough enough to survive. It presents itself as willing good for the other, but its "I know what is best for you" attitude introduces a coercive and even tyrannical note in our lives. All the repressed aggression returns by another route. Under the guise of offering help, it exerts an inflexible control over us.

The second danger is to find ourselves overwhelmed by our hate, identified with it, unable to hold onto any possibility to forgive. We are conquered on the inside by the enemy we are fighting on the outside. We now want to bring to others all the hurt, injustice, and meanness that we have suffered from them. We become what we hate. The danger now doubles. In addition to our original anger at others, we turn intense hostility upon ourselves. *They* have failed us and *we* have failed our own ideals. We now hate self as well as other. We want to be forgiving, but instead we seek vengeance. We condemn in ourselves the murderous thoughts racing through our minds, the violent images inflaming our emotions. We pound ourselves unmercifully, ridiculing our broken resolve, accusing ourselves of hypocrisy. We scorn our own faith as false. We now hold ourselves in contempt.[7] Overcome by our own faults, we reject the person we are or big parts of it. We beat on ourselves like a poor weak, defeated animal.

A favorite means of clubbing our frail self is to make overstrenuous resolves, to take on burdens that are too heavy for us as penances for our faults or as proofs of our will to do better. In fact, however, making such grandiose plans for ourselves merely indulges this same aggression, by asserting our own power to do anything if we "could just make up our minds to it." Of course, reality soon punctures these inflated schemes. Then we call down on our heads even more harsh judgments and more self-revilement.[8] Such attacks only breed more hate of ourselves and the others who initially occasioned the attacks. Bad turns into worse.

Prayer opens us up to all sorts of negative aggression. We feel speechless fury at the irreversible events in life, events that seem senseless, cruel, and cause deep suffering, events that arouse our deepest fear and anger. Death stuns us still in the loss of a dearly loved person, the painful illness of a child, the sudden accident that wipes out a life or maims it. We sit numb, horrified, grieving that we cannot bring life back or even assuage the suffering.

World events only magnify this kind of personal shock. The holocaust against the Jews, the mass murders of Cambodians, the thousands trapped in Russian Gulags defy our imagination. Only the images of faith can make these facts of horror graspable. Evil reigns; its personification, the devil, triumphs. Even those facts that should be intelligible, because they are traceable to human causes, can elude our understanding. We can barely take in the condition of the despoiled persons of our world — those deprived of mind because of poverty, because of no education or bad education or the abuse of parents, those whose sanity trickles away like sand in water, those who have been left to rot in public hospitals after fighting and being crippled in their nation's wars, those denied the dignity and independence that employment brings. All of these persons can trace their suffering to the malice, stupidity, cruelty, or neglect of other persons, to social systems, and to institutions that breed sickness, pain, and death. Even the facts behind that terrifying waste of human lives seem so remote, so complicated, so hard to get at that we cannot see how to understand and do something about them.

Once we open to it suffering can overwhelm us. Prayer assures us of that opening. Because aggressive anger is one of the most basic human defenses against suffering, the more we pray the more we can expect to find the inchoate anger in ourselves loosened, accessible, and pouring from us. Why does God allow this suffering, we want to know. How can God be loving and let these things happen? How can a just God permit millions of people to be violated in soul and body? A tide of rage threatens to drown us. Our faith runs the risk of being engulfed by our anger. Under the pressure of such aggression, we can easily stop praying altogether.[9]

What then should we do with aggression in prayer? *Use it.* We need our aggressive energies in order to pray and to go on praying in the midst of suffering, to go past discouragement, to go past conflicting feelings, and to get over the loss of the quickening imagery on which our prayer so much depends. Aggression helps us hold on in the imageless dark when we hear no answer and feel no result. Aggression provides the energy to persevere so that we can disidentify our insistence on linking prayer with pleasant moods, so that we can penetrate further into the dark origins of our yearning for God, no longer coming to God simply for what God can do for us. With the energy of aggression we can come to endure the chastening, focusing, and intensifying of our desire to seek God for who God is, in God's otherness, in God's majesty.

Our aggressive energies in our prayers will strengthen our prayers and will toughen them to survive the disillusionment of unfulfilled wishes and broken projections. Evil exists and will exist — our image of God as removing all suffering breaks and falls apart on that hard fact. Death takes those we love — our image of a God who will somehow prevent their dying must itself die. Aggression helps us endure and helps us risk letting go, surrendering all into God's hands.

Unless we lose our images of an endlessly yielding God who will perform all our miracles for us, we will lose instead the whole venture of praying and what it means. We need aggression to face this loss and to hold on. Think of St. Teresa of Avila, who writes that she prayed for twenty years without answer. Think of Lady Julian of Norwich who writes that she waited for fifteen years for understanding of a vision. Think of Nicholas of Flüe whose vision so destroyed all his notions of the Godhead that it took him decades to assimilate the vision through attempts to paint it and to meditate upon what he had painted.[10] We need aggression to hold on when no answer comes. We need even more aggression to survive the answer that does come. Our projected images stretch before us like stairs that lead toward God and then stop short of their goal. We need aggression to mount or descend those stairs and then to be able to wait at their end to see what God has to show us.

For example, we bring to God a situation that arouses our anger. We cannot stand the brutalization of millions under dictatorships. We are shocked by the pictures of the boat people, Asian or Cuban or whoever. Everywhere we see a modern series of images of the Disasters of War that makes Goya's look tame and understated by comparison.[11] We voice our anger, our horror, and then entrust it to the Lord. A change of vision may take place. We see our enemies captured by forces of evil. Like the early Christians, we find images that separate us from our personal anger and that disidentify us from our personal version of the villainy. We see those who persecute us held captive, victims themselves as much as those they victimize. We see that we all fall under the sway of principalities and powers that breed unkindness and injustice. In the midst of murderous hatred, we pray that God's goodness may somehow arise and be felt. In the midst of a gaping deprivation of goodness and truth, one that breeds waste and wickedness, we pray that God's presence may enter. We entrust to God not only our anger but our envy; we put it there to be absorbed in the plenitude of being. Into God's holding, we place our yawning insecurity, to be gathered up like holes in a row of knitting. We bury our thrusts for power over others in God's mightiness. We disidentify ourselves from it, but we do not deny it or any other part of our aggression. We no longer fear nor condemn our aggressive anger or scandalized shock or envy or drive for power, but release all of it into God's will. We then surprise ourselves to discover that anger sometimes expresses love, that most of our aggressive reactions speak one way or another of caring for others.

Our anger at the evil in the world, natural and man-made, is sometimes so large that we can accuse God of not hearing, not caring, not bothering to respond to our prayers. But when we no longer identify with it, when we can stand aside and look at it for what it is, it can lead us to more solemn meditations on evil and God's actual response to it.

Scripture is rich with examples of the way God enters into our suffering in the face of evil. God weeps with Rachel at the slaughter of her little ones and with Mary at the cross. In Jesus, God knows the assault of temptation, not just minor bedevilings, but cosmic ones — the temptation to take away all hunger and insecurity, but at the loss of worship of God; to secure peace in the world, but at the cost of no longer putting God first; to guarantee divine faithfulness, but at the expense of recognizing God's holy otherness. These temptations are among the most besetting human visions and among the most persistent fantasies of human security. These self-evidently desirable goals bid for Jesus's first allegiance with compelling logic.

Even though Jesus renounces these assaults, confiding his entire trust in God, he lives in the company of evil for the rest of his life, along the frontier of evil, as Karl Barth puts it, subject to its constant offensive warfare. The Pharisees tempt him to prove his power. His mother tempts him to put his ties to her before his doing God's work. His disciples tempt him to despair of human frailty, with their sleepiness in the face of his vigil, their doubting in the face of his affirmation, and their denial and betrayal in the time of his suffering and death. Finally his own disgrace and death tempt him in his human person to despair of God's intention. Here again, as Barth puts it, the good will of God is for the moment indistinguishable from the evil will of humanity and the world and Satan. Jesus voluntarily enters into all these temptations and feels their full force. In each instance he turns his face toward God and willingly puts his fate in God's hands, even when, as at Gethsemane, his own will seeks another direction.[12]

The great resource and purpose of our aggression is willingly to put our fate, no matter how good or bad, into God's hands, to deposit all of our most consciously and vigorously registered reactions into our prayers. As with our fear, we must accept the contradictions of our aggression. We must see that bringing our love and joy and ease to God means also to accept his presence in our suffering and emptiness, and that finding him means accepting him too in our bold actions, our determinations, our vigorous pursuit of purpose and truth. In one way or another, to one degree or another, our prayer will lead us into filled places and lonely places, in any of which we can be convicted of our bad faith, our despair, and our certainty that hateful forces must triumph over us. But everything changes when we assent in our energetic aggressive way to God's presence. Aggression allowed in prayer equips us to risk being foolish for God, makes us willing to look ridiculous in public, and allows us to go with what we believe. We discover the nerve to fail in the service of a daring loyalty to the God who has touched us here.[13]

By bringing us into touch with our aggression, prayer gives us another view of the divine. The God we meet this way is disclosed as aggressive, assertive, commanding, brusque. God says: Here is life. Take it. Seize the day. Accept the love given you. God's wrath no longer threatens us with endless blame. We no longer threaten ourselves with unremitting guilt. God's wrath becomes a daring presentation of life freed of coaxing, wheedling, and bribing. God's wrath becomes the refusal to coerce our choices or to choose for us. We may feel ourselves relentlessly hounded to choose life. Why? Because wherever we turn there is grace. But as with all gifts, even the supreme one of grace can be refused. Brought to the center of life and made free by our aggressions of the harrassments of both good and evil, we have the choice now to take up or put down the love to which these energies have brought us.

There is no mistaking this place of choice to which we have been brought now. Because it is our aggressions which have delivered us to this confrontation with love, our feelings are deeply involved. We are not in a wobbly, uncertain state. We do not feel pulled in a hundred directions at the same time. For once, with all the vigor of a soul sure of its strengths, we know the magnetic attraction of love as a way of life. Now we can pray the paradoxical prayer that welcomes danger and frustration, because it is only through such obstacles that goodness and love can be fully glimpsed. Now we can even meditate upon death, that most dangerous and frustrating of all our obstacles, and prepare ourselves to seize the fullness of our finitude, not with a defiant Epicureanism but with gratitude for how much we have while we still have it.[14] That is what the aggression opened up by our prayer has made possible.

It is a heady place we have come to. We will never be the same after this experience. Now we are living in our defining element, love. Here, as the Russian philosopher S.L. Frank says, we have our being. This is where what Frank calls "the perfection and purity of the inner life" is achieved, and each of us finds his or her own "special perfection . . . unlike any other. . . . " Achieving such a state carries with it some extraordinary conditions.

> No human judgment is possible here since it is both incompetent and objectless; though two men may be doing apparently the same thing, it *is not* the same thing, does not mean the same thing in relation to the unique reality which is being judged — i.e. in relation to the spiritual level reached by their personality, to the degree of its perfection or imperfection, purity or impurity. Therefore the commandment not to judge others, but to judge only ourselves is not merely a moral injunction: it is an expression of a moral standpoint based upon the true understanding of the ontological nature of things. It is impossible to judge correctly when the subject of judgment is hidden from us and is individually unique.

The thrust of Frank's understanding of Christian ethics is that "the human personality as such is not subject to a human tribunal, is outside its competence." We can judge actions, but not personalities; "man's personality, the only sphere where true good and evil are realized, is not subject to anyone's judgment except its own and God's."[15] And so, even in the face of the suffering, greed, and destruction we see all around us and our own powerlessness to do anything much about it, we continue to pray. We know our own strengths and weaknesses and know that when we put our aggressions well at the center of our praying energies, we greatly increase our strengths and diminish our weaknesses. We are in the sphere where good and evil can be dealt with directly, as central values in our lives.

In the deliverance into love to which our aggressions have brought us in prayer, we must reexamine and reorganize our values. We must match one gift with another, God's grace with that gracefully lived life which is a loved life. We do not relinquish our moral values, but we see, in Frank's words, that "there is something which is still more valuable, namely, the living human personality with its needs, its craving for happiness, peace, satisfaction and for a *personal* understanding and justification of life."[16] When we not only see that that is so, but insist upon it in the inner depths of our being, we can live the life of love, we can gather up our aggressions and live with them and love with them. And living and loving with full acknowledgement of our aggressions, we can see the importance — the enlarged, not the diminished stature — of the persons for whom we pray. Held in the personhood of God they are larger, stronger, and more enduring than suffering, greed, destruction, or any of their own limitations. We do not judge them but use our aggressions to love and pray for them.

The Christ we follow is the Savior, not the judge. The look of love we turn upon ourselves is the saving one, not the judging one. We go out to ourselves and to others in the aggressive fullness of our being where we meet everyone, and not the least among them ourselves, in our identities as loving *men* and, loving *women*.

Chapter Eight
SEXUALITY
and PRAYER

Are these the most unlikely of subjects to be linked together or the most fitting? Generally we think of praying to God as lying outside of sexual experience. Perhaps there still linger in our mind the traditional prayer instructions to banish all sexual images while praying, lest their excitement interfere with our concentration upon God.[1] Or it may be that our images of God encourage a pre-oedipal identity of self in non-sexual terms — as the child of God, or as a creature, soul, or spirit, altogether outside male and female characteristics. Still, we live this life as sexual beings who experience our sexuality at every stage of our lives, knowing as a result many shades, intensities, mutings, and satisfactions precisely as the males and females we are. How can this central human experience be excluded from praying?

When we read the giants of prayer, we discover how frequently they include sexuality in their visions of God and in their metaphors and allegories of relation to God. The highly charged language of the Song of Songs is everywhere in their writings. The abiding rhetoric in Teresa of Avila and John of the Cross, Origen and Gregory of Nyssa, Bernard of Clairvaux and William of St. Thierry, gathered from the Old Testament source, is of sexual embrace.[2] But there is also a vision of a praying being as a nursling at its source in the bosom of God, here made unmistakably maternal. Brother Lawrence calls God "His King" who greets the sins he has committed with such kindness that he feels like a favored child who knows such an "inexpressible felicity" that he dares to call the source of his joy "the breasts of God." The author of *The Art of Conversing with God,* Father Boutauld, experiences God as both maternal and paternal: "You hold me on your knees as a Mother holds her only child and embraces it tenderly in the transports of her love; . . . you hide me in your bosom as a beloved nursling; . . . you carry me in your arms as a Father carries his son before he is able to walk." St. John of the Cross writes of God weaning us from his milk. Julian of Norwich sees "God almighty" as "our kindly Father" and at the same time "God all-wisdom" as "our kindly Mother." Thérèse of Lisieux effects the most startling and fearless display of emotion in announcing her betrothal and subsequent marriage to the Lord, whose riches of grace then devolve upon her much as any husband or wife of that time was dowered with his or her spouse's property. More daring still is Elizabeth of the Trinity's aggressively sexual metaphor: "I deliver myself to him like a prey. . . . Master, take me, take all of me."[3] John Donne's famous sonnet, "Batter my heart, three person'd God," crosses over the usual sexual boundaries to express the same passion. Donne likens the Lord, in his paradoxical style, to a glassblower who breaks him into pieces to make him "new" and an invader who must expel the usurper who occupies his soul. The final image is intensely sexual: there is no freedom or purity in this love except through their opposites —

> Take mee to you, imprison mee, for I
> Except you 'enthrall mee, never shall be free,
> Nor ever chast, except you ravish mee.[4]

Our contemplative concentration must include our sexuality just as our sexuality must include our contemplative life. Prayer brings within earshot and comprehension the primary speech about who we are. Our sexuality is, after all, right at the center of our being. Young or old, celibate or active, married or single, with or without children, we live as men and women and we pray as men and women. In prayer, our sexuality will voice itself in the concrete ways of bodily urges, emotional impulses, and visions of our own and of the opposite sex.[5]

As we pray more, we listen to and hear more sides to our sexuality. We discover that there is no one model of what a man or a woman should be in their sexual selves. There are many sides to sexual identity. Thus the male emerges in a woman and the female emerges in a man, for we bring to prayer the fundamental drive to find all of ourselves and to be met in all of ourselves. Our urges to take possession, to yield, to enter, and to hold are all gathered into the basic urge to be found acceptable. The images we project upon God give valuable clues to the parts of ourselves we are struggling to accept and have others accept. We find among these projections sexual images for God, while at the same time we are aware of the inadequacy of the simple sexual identification of God as one sex or another, or even as androgynous. God cannot be reduced to human characteristics even though coming to us in terms of our humanity, which of course not only includes but stresses the sexual. God has all being, not just more being. Enlarging our understanding of human resources — recognizing that our sexuality is both more subtle and varied, both more masculine and more feminine than we thought — enlarges our understanding of the source of those resources.

The fullness of being must include the feminine as well as the masculine. We have inherited a language in which *mankind* does not mean *malekind,* and *Lord* does not mean mastery over life in an exclusively male way. To be God the Father does not exclude qualities which psychological perception helps us understand are as matriarchal as they are patriarchal. Without turning the Trinity into a quaternity by adding Mary to the Godhead, we must deepen our understanding of the role of the mother in the life of Christ and in the nature of the divine. This requires a much larger accommodation of the feminine images and components of sexuality than we have been used to. Boehme is a good example of one whose prayers are drawn to the forceful effect of the feminine in his image of Sophia. This incarnation of wisdom is both an emanation and a dwelling place of God's Spirit. In her is revealed God in all his wandering depth. She is a being of wonder, a mirror of divinity in which the Spirit of God beholds itself, as well as an eye that sees. The way to Christ is through union with her, thus placing the feminine mode of being at the very center of redemption.[6]

The figure of Beatrice of Nazareth, the great medieval Dutch mystic, reveals an important paradox of being, often associated symbolically with the feminine. On the one hand she was a major figure in the history of the *Frauenbewegung* in the Netherlands, a leader among those pious women who revolted everywhere in Europe against the narrow traditions which confined them to the cloisters and in the world to a subordinate and silent role, withholding from them the benefits of literacy and learning as well as any active part in the contemporary spiritual revivals of the Benedictines and the Dominicans. With tremendous power, these women threw off such constrictions and created a new way of life, emancipated from home and cloister. Beatrice was one such woman. Yet paradoxically, like Donne's battered heart, she found still more freedom in submission to God. Devoted to regular prayer, to study and to teaching, given to charitable works, she stands out in her annunciation of a particular way, the individual way each person must find for herself or himself. She asserts her power against collective religious form only to offer her power in service to her Lord. She affirms the particular religious way of each individual yet keeps hidden, as if of no consequence, the particulars of her own remarkable life. She vividly exemplifies characteristics associated with feminine symbolism — focus on the freedom to indulge her own particularity, while shunning absolute license; rigorous discipline, while eschewing absolute obedience to a rule; freedom from slavish adherance to tradition, while showing her absolute delight in building up a cultural and spiritual atmosphere in which life could be expanded to its full human sensibilities. Hers was a choice neither of sheer animal survival nor of intransigent asceticism. She was herself, her own feminine self, in a world that was not notable for its friendliness to a woman in religion, much less an independent one. By this insistence on finding her own way toward God, from the particular self she was, Beatrice shows us ways to admit our sexuality into our prayers.[7]

Most things we tend to leave out of praying are those that frighten us, embarrass us, or make us ashamed. Sexuality needs to be faced and included in just those particular terms, with just those special variations that insist upon our individuality. God loves all of us, and therefore our sexual lives, too. So we must bring to prayer the excitements, the wonders, the confusions, and the bruises that make up our lives in this area, just as much as we bring the issues and problems of spirit and soul.

Our prayers may take very simple forms. We may remember praying as a girl that we might be well-liked by boys, that we might grow pretty, or as a boy, that we might be noticed and thought attractive by girls. We may pray in puzzlement over why our body does not seem to work correctly, wondering why we cannot seem to enjoy sex. Though we may enjoy sexual activity, perhaps it does not come easily. We may not find natural release in orgasm. We may need to pray about our fear of getting or sustaining erections, or the threat we feel in our minds about old age taking away our potency. We may need to pray about our worry about aging, wrinkling, sagging, fearful that we may lose our desirability. We may find ourselves praying not to be pregnant, or please above all to be made pregnant. Or we may pray mournfully because we no longer can be made pregnant when that phase of life is finished, or we may say prayers of thankful relief because of it. We may pray out of a guilt we feel at wanting sex too much, making sexuality serve for all forms of contact and communication. We may pray for release from a sexual desire to which we feel enslaved. We may pray in confusion and conflict that we prefer the opposite sex to our own and want to identify ourselves as a member of that group, that as women we really want to be men, or as men we want to be women. We may pray out of guilt because our sexual life is too singular, too self-enclosed. We may pray in desperation of ever finding a sexual partner who arouses both passion and tenderness in us. We may pray in thanks for the miracle of joining with the partner we have, for the deep satisfaction of body and soul he or she brings. We may pray prayers full of attack against our body, of shame for the way it is shaped or misshaped, for its too great size or too little, its fatness or scrawniness, its flatness or bulges. We may pray in dismay that we have rejected a part of our body, in effect disowned it so that it becomes a symbol for our self-revilement.

We may discover our sexual life has been all but totally blocked off, lived only mentally at best, with a sort of passing acknowledgement of the fact that of course we are a man or woman, though in fact we have never lived below the neck in terms of what it feels like to be this man or that woman. We simply avoid the issue, dressing in camouflaging clothes, skipping over body urges, checking fantasy before it arises, cutting the plant of our sexuality at its root. Prayer opens up this whole issue to us. We may find that our sexuality is full of grief over a lost or deceased partner. The grief, painful as it is then, must be spoken. The specific ways we remember that person's body, smell, taste, and touch must be acknowledged. We must bring it all into our prayer.

Prayer offers us our best recourse in the world of sexuality: to be particular just as we are and to confide all these matters into God's keeping, to gather up in the great container of prayer all those bits of sexual worry, desire, fear, and hope and carry them to God, depositing them, entrusting them, securing them in God's care.

By bringing all this to prayer, we open ourselves to our own sexual life as we register God's participation in it, a participation that we experience in different ways. We find a new release from a compulsion, discover a sudden insight into a problem, develop a continuing wonder at the goodness of sexual experience, and find a healing of our guilt. Bringing all the sides of our bodily sexuality to God in prayer directs us to one good end — gratitude. We have gratitude for the body we have, a body that we can come to accept despite its imperfections; gratitude for the sexual currents we have felt, whatever they are or have been; gratitude for the desires we have satisfied and even for some that have been left dangling. Our gratitude sometimes opens us still further, to discover that our sexuality may be more than we assumed and less than we feared.

Prayer that includes sexual themes makes us inspect our sexuality and register what it is and what it is not. We sort through its tumble of affect, impulse, and emotion and register all our different modes of feeling. We discover a restless urge to activity — to poke into and investigate things, to penetrate, to make contact, and enter into our sexual world. Or we find a compelling need to draw into ourselves, to have something carried out upon ourselves, to pull in, to reach up, to lead further and further into ourselves, magnetically to attract and make something happen. These urges are traditionally divided up into male and female attitudes and procedures. But, when we contemplate our sexuality in prayer, these urges show themselves to belong to all of us, men and women alike, in different degrees and patterns, in different kinds of emphasis. What prayer can lead us to is the seeing and accepting of these bodily urges as wonderful parts of our humanity.[8] If we revile them instead, the urges that claim us against ourselves will exist only negatively, as rapacious urges to rip apart or as humiliating urges to be smashed.

Prayer makes a space simply to look and to contemplate, and thus to free our ego from compulsively controlling these urges, often without thought or understanding, through the mechanical use of a religious precept or moral code that marks them as bad. In the freeing space of prayer, we can no longer pretend that they do not exist. We no longer are reduced to repressing them or just diving into them unthinkingly. The alternative route that prayer encourages is to see and to offer, to accept what is there and give thanks for it and open our living out of sexuality as a central part of our being to God's care.

Sexuality operates on an emotional plane and a spiritual plane as well as a physical one.[9] The movement prayer must take on these levels is the invariable one — to open and to inspect what is there and offer all to God's encompassing love, even the violent problems, the wrenching losses, the neurotic twistings to which our sexuality so often falls victim. On an emotional level, we experience our sexual drive in images of sexual activity in the parts or the whole of the person that attracted us. These images exert a numinous fascination in us. That fascination comprises one of life's most moving experiences and should not be excluded from our prayers. Emotionally, we idealize these persons, these parts, and these states of being and feel compelled to actual contact with them. We want to rub up against them, to have them in our possession, to get physical hold of the emotional value they personify. On this level, we find a sudden enlargement in the meetings of the body and the emotions aroused by another. Our psyche is thrown wide open to the touch of otherness.

We are pulled right out of ourselves toward the other. We feel summoned by this fresh evidence of otherness to come toward it, to mix with it, to know it, to behold it. Caught up in such an emotional attraction, it is hard to know whether this otherness really exists in the other person or personifies part of ourselves. We only know its compelling attraction, all the more forceful because less tangible than our physical drives. We want to make this glimpse of otherness real to ourselves by touching it. Such an attraction must be brought into our prayers — spoken, reviewed, handled, and offered. Just to run with the attraction or run away from it avails nothing. The first option leaves us lost in the turmoil of the emotional drive; the second denies us access to the splendor of the emotional drive. The real alternative is to bring all of it into our conversation with God, which amounts to sacrificing our identification with it in order to see it and claim it for what it is and to allow ourselves, where we should be, to be claimed by it.

On the spiritual level, the attraction of otherness widens, deepens, and takes on its true weight. In meetings of body and emotions with another, the soul is thrown open to a more direct encounter with otherness itself, as there beholding *us*.[10] Something additional enters into our sexual meetings; through the physical and emotional bond there effected the soul is stirred, changed, and sometimes marked for life. This profound experience cannot be ignored. The particular presence of the other person takes on more and more importance as our perception grows of another being, living its own life in its own right. In addition, something within ourselves demands attention with more and more force. We discover a greater fullness in our own sexuality. As men, we come to know feminine attitudes in ourselves; as women, we claim masculine potentialities and begin to actualize them. Any man who has taken the trouble to examine his own sexuality — the range of his bodily impulses and emotional drives — will confess he wants some of the time to be found by a strong woman, to be taken into her in order to be held, and, if more daring, will admit he wants to begin to give by receiving, yielding passively to a woman's lead, giving himself up to her direction, to be seen as he is without guile or disguise or protection. This motion on her part will stir his passion as deeply as do his own more initiating actions. Any woman will admit to herself, if she takes the time, that sometimes she wants to assert her lovingness in modes of taking, piercing, growing inwardly into her lover's body and being, summoning his responses by her gestures and postures in modes of commanding that arouse her own responses as fully as her receptive actions do. Both partners seek ways to bring together the otherness of the masculine and feminine within themselves.[11] They want to find a way to join other opposites they have in common as well. They want to include aggressiveness in the embrace of love. They want their love to hold onto, to be held within their combative energies, the vigorous claiming and asserting, with each other. They want the giving and nothing-held-back-offering of self to other which love can know.

It must be stressed here that the offering of self we make is only possible because we have become so conscious of having a self. The growth of our understanding of self ("self-consciousness" in the best possible sense of that phrase) can be hastened and deepened as we move through the bodily element to the emotional and spiritual dimensions of our sexual identity. It is by no means a mechanical process, in which stage succeeds stage with oiled precision. But it is a necessary development. As the English philosopher John McTaggart understood so well, the defining element of love is union with another person, and that union is not possible without a heightened degree of self-consciousness.[12] In the assent to self that this form of consciousness represents, we make the offering of self to other which may call forth an equal and opposite offering from the other to our self. What has started, perhaps, as an agreeable meeting with a person — an intense appreciation of somebody's eyes or nose or muscles or bosom or legs, a response of delight to a personality type — ends as a joining of persons. A random touching of bodies may lead to that touching of selves where we discover the crossroads of the human and the divine.

The spiritual dimension of sexuality, built upon and never excluding the bodily and emotional parts, expands sexuality to emphasize the mark of otherness in this intimate touching of selves. Perhaps that is one reason why sexual metaphors reflecting the world of the flesh turn up so often as the major language of the great mystics to describe their most rapturous meetings with God, meetings that defy words because of their acute thrust. They encompass fervor that, paradoxically, goes so far beyond the flesh. The spiritual dimension of our sexuality is what comes clear to us as we bring our sexual needs, worries, and hopes into our conversations with God. We speak about them to God; we lay them open to God. We offer them as something that we care about greatly, as we do about those things that most delight us or confuse us, frighten us or astound us.

When we come to prayer we must come with all of our sexuality, too — as a woman praying over her sexual concerns, as a man beset by sexual fears, as a person afflicted by perversions or insatiable desires or no discoverable libido, as a deeply satisfied lover, as one with secret hopes for a true and lasting love that has not yet come. In sexuality, as in all else, we allow our utter dependency on God to come to the fore. Thus the images of God as mother rise spontaneously to our lips. We are held in God's lap and comforted at God's breast. The images of God as spouse and lover come easily as we seek to be taken into God's love and to open to it.

The language of primary speech is not timid in its movements of love. Its metaphors are boldly textured in the colors of bodily rapture, instructed by the example of such distinguished practitioners of the past as John of the Cross, on fire with "the living flame of love," and Bernard of Clairvaux, to whom the interior presence of God was honey on the tongue. Everywhere in this timeless world of "unmeasured inward shining," as the fourteenth-century Jan Van Ruysbroeck called it, there are

the marks of "delectable inclination," a "nakedness" in which we "lose
... observation and perception of all things" and are "formed again and
transfused with a single clarity."[13]

We come to prayer, of course, as men and women of our own time.
No matter how thoroughly we may be caught up in the imagery of the
saints and the mystics, no matter how much we may welcome the rhetoric
of kings and queens and peers of the spiritual realm, in our fantasies, our
world is not that of the Middle Ages or the Renaissance. We can only go
so far with Teresa of Avila's adulation of "His Majesty" or the vassal-
to-Lord bondage of a medieval worshiper. The few monarchs we know
anything about in our world are constitutional, and absolute power has
the ugly connotations of Fascist and Communist dictatorship for us.
When we welcome our Lord in our devotions it must inevitably be in the
homely raiment of everyday life. That is where we make common cause
with the maternal deity of Julian of Norwich and the romantic lover of
the nineteenth-century apostles of prayer. Nor should we feel in any way
uneasy because our God wears such ordinary clothing. We can only come
as we are to prayer. To come in disguise, to insist upon the trappings of
the centuries of chivalry and monasticism, however comforting it may be
to be that child in us that still likes to dress up in make-believe finery,
is to run the risk of falsifying ourselves in just those exchanges where we
should be most honest with ourselves. The authority we meet in such
encounters may not be God at all, but only our superego trotted out in
doublet and hose.

The opposite extreme is no better. To see God only in the squalors
of our world is to keep Christ forever on the cross, or worse, in a
perpetual scourging. The divinity we are privileged to meet in prayer is,
as divinity surely always has been, a thorough reflection, among other
things, of every aspect of life as human beings know it. For us, that must
mean every known rictus of suffering in which, to its dubious distinction,
the twentieth century has specialized. But it must also mean the joy of
this time, the pleasure, for example, that this of all centuries has taken
in those who in earlier eras were in effect thrown back, as not worthy of
life — the handicapped of all kinds, the so-called retarded, the victims
of physical and psychological and spiritual illness in whom we have
found so much to admire, with whom we have discovered so much to
share. God is not only in these newly formed outlanders of our society

but also in the pleasure we take in welcoming them, in learning from them, in loving them and being loved by them, in finding far reaches within ourselves from which love can spring — and does.

This is where the language and imagery and experience of sexuality is so useful to prayer, and, even more, where it is necessary. In the physical experience of our sexuality at its best, we know the marvel of sheer play. Gratification will be in it, of course, and the satisfaction of an animal urge that far from demeaning us by its association with goats and monkeys, for example, asserts the extraordinary range of our appetites and the equipment we are given to satisfy them. But our sexual play sometimes reaches such a vibrant outgoing delight that we can understand in it some of the absolute joy that divinity must feel in coming toward us.

We have our own splendid parallels in our lives to the care a mother cat shows for her kittens or a father goose for his whole family. We couple often enough with the magnificent determination to create our own families in the image and likeness, not of our bodies, but of the love that brings them together. But even this is not quite the high experience of sexuality to which, as Rabelais reminds us with such fervor, the Old Testament gives the name of mutual solace. In ancient Israel the bringing together of man and woman in marriage took precedence over all else, even the defense of the holy land. A couple was given a year to enjoy its new state — the graces of its love — before military or other service was required of the husband.[14]

In that construction of love, sexuality finds its special sanction and primary speech one of its greatest sources of appeal. In that reading of married love, we know why what has much too often been an unworthy part of ourselves, our sexual identity, has been for the mystics the most cherished means to explain who they are and what they are.

Sexuality is without question much of the time only a means, not an end, for the mystics. To them, as to us as well, sexuality has a large symbolic life. But only the smallest and most self-denying of imaginations would confine it to the symbolic, whether for the celibate mystic or the active husband or wife. All are lovers. All are tutored in their love by the sexuality that defines a center of their being. And thus all are brought to their prayers, and made more in their prayers, by their sexual desire.

Chapter Nine
PRAYING
for OTHERS

All prayer is social. We discover this when we pray for others. When our prayers are of intercession we enter the zone of mutuality between people, freely admitting how much we depend on others being there before us. We mean that in two senses. First, we must really see those persons, catch them in the mind's eye. Then, the images in which we pray must be understood to stretch back into the human past. We rely on countless other persons' experiences and efforts to speak about their experience in the words and symbols of human culture. We draw upon the accumulated wisdom of the churches, their storehouses of images and rituals that show us the many different ways to pray.[1] From a more recent past, when we pray we draw upon specific images, words, and postures taught us by our parents or teachers. From the very beginning of prayer, we see that even our most intimate inner life is inhabited by other people and what we have made of what they have shown us.

When we pray for others, we not only seek something for them but we also acknowledge our dependency on them. We only achieve being through relationships with others, with other real persons. A glimpse of this mystery and its fundamental reality appears in the image of the Trinity. The internal being of God exists as relationship, a love so vital and vividly expressed that only the image of persons in unceasing connection to each other can capture it. Jesus indicates that this sort of interconnectedness both precedes his birth and survives after his death as a principal way to link us to God through him. "He always lives to make intercession for [us]," as the words of Hebrews put it.[2]

Whom then do we pray for? What is this zone of mutuality we share with others, on which our being depends? Who intercedes for whom? The whole society of persons who make up our world comes quickly to mind, their hurts and hopes, their causes and failures.[3] We speak of them to God; we lift them up to God; we entrust them to God, and often enough they do the same for us.

We pray for those we love because we must. We know that our love is not powerful enough to protect them from all harm, from all illness, from all evil, from death. Our love is not omnipotent. Our care for them, our insistence that they must have a good life, a full life, a life lived from the center of themselves, forces us to intercede with God on their behalf. By ourselves we cannot guarantee them much. We cannot even prevent our own faults from hurting them. We cannot restrain our own strong hopes and pressures so that they can find and live their own idea of the good life instead of the one we have ordained for them. When we recognize these limiting effects of our love, it is that very love for our children, our dear friends, our husband or wife that impels us beyond ourselves to confide their souls into God's keeping. Praying for them changes our love from a closed to an open hand, from a hand that tightly holds them under rein to one that holds them loosely. Praying for them makes us supple and flexible in our love for them.

We learn to pray for those we dislike and avoid, for those we hate and fear, for our enemies. Such prayer shifts our attention from all the things others have done to us or neglected to do that so wounded or enraged us, to focus on what it is in ourselves that permits others to acquire such power over us, the power to put us, in effect, in the hell of anger, or dismay, or insecurity, or fear. Prayer for them directs us to the antecedent attitudes or conditions of personality in ourselves that deliver us over into others' power. For example, some people make us angry with seemingly incessant demands. In our minds, we accuse them of never doing their own work, of always manipulating others to do it for them. We feel used and resent it. When we try talking directly to such a person, the situation almost always goes from bad to worse. Our candor is met with denials. An ugly atmosphere develops. Tension mounts. Simply avoiding the person is not an option, for we work or live together and cannot run away. When once again that person asks us to do something, at the very least we explode inwardly — and then feel miserable about our response and look for ways to justify it.

To pray for a person who does such things to us includes investigating what attitude in ourselves permits anyone so to get under our skin, why it never occurs to us, for example, to say no to their aggrandizing requests.[4] Instead, we close up like a fortress in our defensive maneuvers — and then we feel besieged. If we did not defend ourselves in such a prickly self-enclosing way, all those demanding strategies and ploys would not get to us. A simple no would suffice; we would not feel attacked and then desperately need to justify our explosive reaction.

Praying for our enemies changes our attitudes toward them. Enemies make us bring light into painful hidden corners of ourselves that we would prefer to leave dark. By trying to put ourselves in another person's shoes, we may discover what we do that so irritates others and makes them dislike us. We hear new voices in our prayer that usually we tune out. We see ourselves from a different angle, one we could not find either by ourselves or with the help of friends. Only enemies can help us here. In this way they are priceless.

How very hard it is to pray for someone we hate or someone whom at a given moment we want so to hurt! It takes a wrestling with demons to eke out a prayer in such circumstances, often from between clenched teeth, and for, of all people, the one against whom we want only revenge! We pray — if we can — that God's goodness will be placed at the center of their actions and attitudes, that God's goodness will work there and flourish.

Praying for our enemies releases within us parts of ourselves that really are our own enemies, forces hostile to our conscious sense of who we are. We admit back into ourselves left-out parts that we want to forget — laziness, petty concerns, our own hostilities, often so generalized we do not even know at what or whom it is we are angry. These are alien parts that do not fit in with our image of ourselves but that nonetheless belong to our identities, such as our poor beginnings or rich beginnings, or highly troubled family background. We come upon hateful parts of ourselves when we want only to vanquish others, to be superior to them, to have everything for ourselves. We find the parts of ourselves that really do not see or in any way respect the individual existence of others.

Praying for our enemies reveals to us how much we need the same intercessory mercy bestowed on the conflicts warring within ourselves.

Intercession leads us to pray for those already dead, both the loved ones and the enemies of our own past. We pray for a father, a mother, a grandmother, or an aunt who loved us and helped us be by really seeing us as we were and rejoicing in our own special personhood, not because it was so superior or gifted, not because it caused such worry or fear, but simply because it was. They were glad in us, glad for what we were, and communicated to us their grateful joy of acceptance at the most basic level. This kind of acceptance makes life exciting because when we are met and greeted in this way we feel real, alive, and delighted to be our very own self. Praying for the souls of such persons, in death as in life, releases into life a fullness of gratitude for their existence. We pray for their joy, their salvation, their immediacy to divine presence, their being-at-the-core in whatever form resurrected life exists for them.

Our prayers extend well beyond our families and friends, to teachers, for example. We pray for those who taught us and summoned us to learn that we might be able to see and respond to what is, to multiple layers of existence, to what matters in life. We can even pray for the grades, the scores that admit us to the next school and the next, and even with strong concern for our job placement or an honored place in society. We pray for those things taught us that bring the highest graces, the greatest interior ease. We pray in hope and in thanks that being will be made open to us, that we will meet life at its center. We pray that those who have made us experience these things will themselves have understood and experienced them and are now living at the center of being where experience and understanding have their source.[5]

In praying for those already dead, we open to our own dying, to the undoing of our own life in its present forms. We give over control and we unravel the cares of this life, quieting down to admit the fears of letting go into the unknown. Praying for the dead makes a bridge in us to the death that awaits us and makes room for our uncertainties and fears. And contemplating death curiously enough calls us into life more fully, to live it right up to the end because we free our energies from the fear of death to the devotion to life.

There may also exist in us now dead parts of ourselves, killed off by the way we have thrust them away from us into the dark. We may dream of corpses. We may realize that we do not respond with lively feeling in a situation that clearly calls for it. Instead we are blank, we are dead. We may have cut ourselves off from our feeling, from our will, or from our memories of our childhood to such an extent that they are all dead — feeling, will, childhood — weighing us down like so many dead weights. Praying for the dead touches the dead parts in ourselves and calls them back into being.

The fact is that some of us have so successfully hidden our true self under layers of pretended reactions and rhetorical compliance to others' expectations that it is all but dead. Praying for the dead may make us reach to this hidden, shut-off core, this germ of ourselves, and uncover it. In prayer we may find a place to be as we really are, safe in God's seeing and keeping.

We may pray for others yet to be met in the future — persons we do not know, situations that have not yet happened. We pray then to be open, receptive, alert, not wasting energy on frivolous details at the periphery of things, but able to concentrate on the center. We pray for persons we may fear to meet — persons of the opposite sex who will draw us into passion, for example, because we have so avoided waking up to our own sexuality. We may pray for persons who are or will be in authority over us, employers for example, those we too often fear or want to defy or to follow slavishly. We can pray to see them as they are and not to identify them with their positions, but to enter together with them a zone of mutual recognition of our shared and essential humanity. We pray for those with whom we cannot make any contact, who seem too different from us in culture, in language, or in point-of-view. We pray to be accessible and not just to close up and turn away from such people.

We pray for those we meet who are suffering or will suffer, that we may be attentive, neither interfering with hasty solutions that really only cut off other persons' displaying to us how deeply they suffer, nor quitting the scene because we cannot stand their pain. Such prayers open unlived parts of ourselves, interceding for easier access for them to our consciousness and thus to our development. We open the windows wide to see what will come in from the outside and what will come out from the inside.

Some philosophers and theologians have doubted the possibility or the usefulness of praying for people and events in the past and, by implication or directly, for those in the future. If we cannot break the time barrier in our reach through finitude to God's timelessness in our compassionate concern for those of the past, how can we any more assuredly reach into present or future events and the people experiencing them? In both cases, we bring our care and concern to the root of being, outside time. God knows in his permanent present what our prayers have been and are and will be. It is no simplification or sentimentalization of faith to assume that the misery of the fifth or fifteenth century, A.D. or B.C., or any other time that has been or is now or will be, can be graced with the intervention of a God who in his timelessness is fully aware of all the prayers that will be offered up in time and of their purposes as well. And so we can in good heart and good mind pray for Christ on the way to the cross or upon it, for Hector being lashed to Achilles' chariot and trampled in the dust behind it, for the victims of the Black Hole of Calcutta and the gas furnaces of Auschwitz, for St. Augustine's toothache and Mozart's unfinished *Requiem*. In one way of speaking, we can say that all time and all space are accessible to us in prayer, and in another way, we can say that there is neither time nor space in prayer.[6]

Prayer enters the non-space, non-time zone, that part of our life that knows no boundaries and partakes of the timelessness of God's eternity. There, each moment exists in a permanent "now," standing out from other moments as all there is. Thus we can pray across limitations of time and space. Our prayers for persons in the past and the future cross barriers of causality to participate in what happened then or will happen in a time and place yet to come. We can pray, therefore, for people and events of the past with the conviction that we actually do enter those past moments that stand out firmly and clearly from an endless collection of shapeless moments. We can pray for Jesus suffering alone in the garden at Gethsemane. We can pray for the martyr facing the lion. We can pray for Peter hanging upside down, crucified, his head bursting with pain. We can pray for a poor woman burned as a witch at the stake. We can pray for an exhausted child laboring twelve hours a day in a nineteenth-century English mill. We can pray for a black man lynched by the Ku Klux Klan. We can pray for the people of Pompeii burned alive in hot lava. We can pray for the stunned and hideously deformed victims of the bombing of Hiroshima. We can pray for the mother watching her child led into a gas chamber at Dachau. We can pray for old persons left unloved, unvalued, in dirty rooms, bad nursing homes, an empty world. We can pray for the child numbed by pain and confusion under the blows of an abusive parent. We can pray for the woman terrified as she is attacked and raped. And we can pray for those in the future who will suffer fear, degradation, pain, loss.

We can pray for the assuagement of their suffering, entering into their moments with our own beseeching for mercy and light and comfort in the midst of horror. We can pray that goodness exist in every such moment, that people cling to it and build it up in the face of evil. We can pray that men and women will seek and find work and be able to feed their children, that they will look and see the wonder of what is given them each day, in the sky, the flowers, their neighbors' faces, their dream-images, in touches of unexpected kindness, in the laughter and the tears of compassion they elicit. We can pray for a blessed death for those we love and those we do not, for those we know and those we do not. We can pray for a softness of heart that can take in what is given and fill up with it. We can pray that persons live at their centers and from their centers, close to the center of divine care, looking for God's presence and wanting it, wanting to go with God's will and knowing the joy of doing so.

Intercessory prayer in this sense is for everyone. It is, for example, for institutions and those in them who make good use of them and those who are hurt and exploited and make bad use of them or are used badly by them. It is for the churches, the official congregations and communities devoted to worship of God, and all the parts of the human family that the churches represent. God's space is the human family, what we are to each other and what we make possible for each other. But too often we crowd God out, or push God into the underground, or break up into scattered bits God's ineffable being so that it is hard to perceive "being" as truly coming from God. We try to destroy being by what we do against each other. We make abundant life meager, mean, and denying of self, our own and others'. The refusal to recognize persons in themselves, as themselves, each in his or her uniqueness, makes the church and our world sick. We must pray for healing and be ready for the surprise of the healing when it comes.[7] It does not come as an institutional triumph. It comes in our sudden recognizing of the person next to us, the person in our neighborhood, our congregation, our place of work, our home, our bed.

Intercessory prayer pulls us into the tow of God's connectedness to everything. We are pulled into a current that shows us nothing is separated from anything else, no one from everyone else. We are in an ocean that flows under everything and through everyone. Not only do we discover the hungry parts of ourselves that we need to feed when we pray for the hungry persons of the world, but we discover the neglected parts of the world through praying into being the neglected parts of ourselves. When we deal with the hating parts of ourselves, we see with sudden clarity how much hate exists in the people around us.

When we pray for the suffering parts of ourselves, we are increasingly wounded by the suffering of others around us. We are like Frau Walker in Albrecht Goes' *The Burnt Offering*, who could not stand the suffering of the Jews under the Nazis one more minute. She thought she knew the excruciating limit when her young, pregnant Jewish neighbor came to her to give away the baby clothes and carriage she had bought for her unborn baby because she knew she would soon be taken to a death camp and the baby killed in her before it could even be born. That night Frau Walker's house is hit in a bombing raid and she voluntarily crawls into the fire and gives herself as a burnt offering for the Jews' suffering. A Jew rescues her. At first she thinks her offering has not been accepted. Only slowly does she learn that it has been accepted and that the offering has become her whole life, a life of service to the Jews. The bush is not consumed. God does not want human sacrifice; God wants us to live fully and to open fully to each other. Praying for the suffering of others leads us to offer our suffering on their behalf, to make our whole life, like Frau Walker's, an offering.[8]

Offering our suffering for others is not an easy way out of our pain. It is, if anything, a guarantee that our pain will continue — with the very considerable amelioration that comes from knowing that the pain has some purpose beyond the struggle for physical existence, some direction and terminus beyond itself. But the risk is great. When we offer any part of ourselves, and especially that fullness of our life which is caught up in our suffering, we leave ourselves exposed as in almost no other way. Whether the suffering we offer up is our own physical pain or the perhaps even greater ache we feel in the face of the pain of those we love, we must know that prayer does not always bring surcease. The pain not only may go on — ours or others' — but it may increase. The tragic textures of life are boldly outlined in this enterprise of prayer.[9]

Three crucial issues should enter our meditations at this point. They make up the triunity of intercessory prayer, an interlocking set of realizations which together amount to the reality principle on which intercessory prayer is founded. The first is in the realm of common sense. Whether or not we offer our suffering for others, the suffering exists and will continue to exist, both our own suffering and others'. If not in this way, then in some other; if not in this part of the body, then in some other; if not to this beloved person, then to some other. Human ingenuity will undoubtedly find ways to eradicate many of the causes of illness. Some of the worst of the terrors that afflict the body will be conquered. But human ingenuity will also find new ways to spoil the earth and corrupt the body. For every cancer of our interior world that we erase or hold in check, we create an equally ferocious one in our exterior world. It is only a simplistic mind, bent on reducing everything to a political or economic determinism, that can be satisfied with an easily identified set of villains to account for the pollution of the outside environment that invariably leads to a contamination of our inside one. Big business bent on profit, big government either in league with big business or indifferent to human suffering — there is the cause of everything. If we must have a facile explanation, which will make it all quickly clear, are not the terms of an ancient theology more satisfactory? Human greed, sloth, pride — will they not go as far to explain things as the comicstrip-like evildoers? One way or the other, the suffering of the body continues and the first of the three units of our triunity must be accepted.

The second is the suffering of the mind. Here again, we have accomplished much to reduce or to appease pain. But the "cure" promised by the use of the word "therapy" in the treatment of the psyche is questionable, as questionable as the modern mythology of science which promised an end to misery, illness, maldistribution of wealth, even the inequality of human talents for so long. What depth psychology, psychiatry, and the various mixings of psychology, religion, philosophy, and social work have been able to accomplish only underlines more strongly the inevitable imbalances that human relations must yield. A true freedom of exchange between persons is a risky one. Candor brings at least some tension, as honest doubts and inevitable disappointments are expressed. That it also assures the possibility of an intimate meeting of persons cannot efface the difficulties that every continued relationship must accept. What is to some people a particular unhappiness is that when they have achieved relationship, accepting its real problems, but also finding its great satisfactions, they still must run into the turmoil caused by all those others who have not accomplished as much. As with bodily ills, those of the psyche can be diminished, and learned to be lived with, but they will not disappear. To expect that particular miracle is to reject the greater miracle of human freedom.

The last of the units of the triunity of prayer is the suffering of the spirit. Here, in the spirit, where we can expect to find the true dimensions of our human self and that encounter with the divine where our humanity finds its defining grandeur, we often find mere bafflement, or worse, nothing. We feel spurred to prayer. We have a sense of a beneficent providence, an intervening deity just waiting to be summoned to come to our aid. And what do we get? Silence. Not only the old familiar headaches, the stomachaches, the well-known anxieties, but this emptiness, here, where we have ardent belief, demonstrable faith. Only that macabre sense of humor which is satisfied with the old jokes about the way God treats his friends — "Look what he did for his son!" — is likely to settle with any ease into this kind of spiritual pain. But easily or uneasily, the pain will continue in some form or another, and all the more as we move from the psyche to the spirit. There will be silence, or confusing answers, or what will seem to us obviously wrong answers to our prayers. Why bother, then? Here, happily, there is an answer, a whole set of answers which can draw us much closer to all those around us, to those for whom we pray, to the God to whom we pray, and to ourselves.

Here is the special test of faith and, in a sense, the special reward of faith. We do not achieve instant sanctity or great worldly success with our faith or prayer. What we can accomplish is something like union with the unity which is at the center of the geometry of suffering, the triunity that we have called the reality principle of prayer. In the case of physical suffering, the first of the three dimensions of the triunity, whether it increases or diminishes in its intensity, we are equipped now to live with it and we are even able to help others to live with it. We have all but precise statistical evidence for this in the lives of the saints and other great witnesses to this sort of intercessory prayer. The same kind of evidence exists for the usefulness of prayer in response to psychological anguish, the second dimension of the triunity. We need not all become Fools for Christ in the tradition of the wandering devout who were for so long supported as holy fools by the Russians among whom they passed their vagabond lives. We do have to emulate their simple trust in constant prayer as an incomparable support to our tense and nerve-jangling days. Whether spoken loud and clear, merely mouthed, or carried within in an assured interior monologue, our recourse to streams of verbal and non-verbal prayer can create a cocoon of assurance around us and around those for whom we offer this holy conversation.[10] It is not magic thinking that will do this for us. It cannot long remain the half-cynical, half-hopeful dartings at God (or whomever) with which so many begin their prayer life. It must be a trusting movement of the heart in which doubt is not so much answered as put aside.

Finally, in the third dimension of the triunity, we come to the province at once of despair and the highest hope, the realm of the spirit. There, we must be absolutely selfless and thoroughly selfish. We must be willing to choose ourselves, knowing all we do about our inadequacy as central channels for God's grace, our unworthiness to pray for anyone and everyone, living or dead, ancient or modern, who may come to our mind as subjects of prayer. We must accept that appointment to grace and prayer with a kind of biblical sense of humor, recognizing that we would not choose ourselves if we were not already chosen. We must choose ourselves not once, but again and again, astonished, perhaps, to find ourselves caught up in such activity, startled to find that we can join the lists with Paul, Augustine, Francis of Assisi, John of the Cross, Thérèse of Lisieux, Schweitzer, Simone Weil, Mother Teresa in India — anyone and everyone who has ever taken seriously the invitation to become an *alter Christus*.[11] We have to be willing to live in some central core of our being with a round, simple naïveté, even the most complicated or would-be-sophisticated among us. The answer to the silence with which our spiritual ardors are so often greeted is in our own audible prayer. The more we are disturbed by our feelings of puzzlement, frustration, and emptiness in the realm of the spirit, the more vigorous and firm, even clamorous, should be our intercessions. The colder the waters, the more ready we should be to jump in.

Sin is the refusal to get our feet wet in the ocean of God's connectedness. Only through the particular entrances offered us do we enter the waters of intercession. We enter through those persons we love, or hate, those concrete incidents of suffering or gladness that happen to us. Who, after all, if we do not, is going to pray for that nasty woman who begrudged us our change when we bought the morning paper? Who besides us at that moment saw her hardness? Who is going to pray for the mailman whose cheerfulness each day, whatever the weather, brightens his customers and makes life more possible? Who will pray for those children who by the simple fact of their abundant smiles, or super-serious determination to walk on top of every wall in our neighborhood, lighten our days when we meet them? Who will reach out in ache and joy to pray for the remarkable old people who bear the physical pain and metaphysical uncertainties of their closing years and months and days with such dignity and such humanity?

Intercessory prayer means discovering we do not have to do it all nor do it all alone. There are others we increasingly come to recognize who also pray for the world — and even for us! We enter the community of all who pray. But we see that we must do what is given only to us to do in those particular daily incidents that occur to us and around us and within us. We increasingly see how particular Christ's intercession was for us. "*This* is my body. *This* is my blood," he said. When we walk or ride in a road and see a man lying there ill, who is the neighbor?

As we pray for those who concretely come across our path, into our road — those within our immediate world and those without, those of the past and those of the future — the whole question of whether our prayers change other people rearranges itself. When we try to pray for others, we are clear we are changed ourselves. We open up, we soften, we put into perspective hurts they have dealt us. We enter their lives now from their point of view instead of exclusively from our own, and as a result we are introduced increasingly to God's point of view, a remarkable vantage point from which to see their lives and our own. The question of causality (did our prayer do this for them?) dissolves in this increasing current of God's interconnectedness with all of us and our intensified awareness of it in all the parts of our lives.

The whole question of who intercedes for whom becomes part of one great current that gathers us into its own course and we begin to experience something of the intermixture of Jesus, the Spirit, and God. We see one God, yet distinct persons. We see that we are distinct persons, yet one, running in the ceaseless flow of God's being in all of us. To pray that God's will be done is to enter and to be increasingly caught up in the current of that will, and to experience an enlargement of our willingness to go forth, to flow, to consent, to correspond. We who thought we were offering prayers of intercession for others come increasingly to realize that the prayers of others — people known and unknown to us, people from the present and from the past, even people in a future yet to come — flow through us and intercede for us. With others and through others we depend upon and accept the flow of God's grace.

We live the meaning of the mystical body of Christ in this inter-connectedness of intercession, where our pleas for others become pleas for ourselves and their pleas for themselves become pleas for us. We know by direct experience that we are, as St. Paul says, members one of another.[13] One further confirmation of this extraordinary fact comes to us if in our development of intercessory prayer we move into the prayer of free association. In it, we bring together whatever names and concerns come to our minds — or to our hearts or souls — as soon as we have selected our first name, our first person, for whom to pray. Others follow in remarkably fast order, in a rich, gladdening discourse with the Spirit, each name suggesting another, and another, and another, directly connected or loosely connected or not connected at all except in our prayer. We do not have to hunt for people, or worry about what may be bothering them, or work at it with any degree of intensity. They will come to us, the people who should be filling our prayers, the needs they have or have had or are likely to have. Some of them may have been absent from our thoughts for years or even decades. Many of them we may have forgotten we ever knew. We will be surprised and occasionally disturbed, but we will almost always feel filled up, enlarged, and supported in ourselves by the experience. Our past and present and future come together here in this procession of the spirit engendered by our prayers. And if we do not make this movement across all the encounters of our lives into a game which we play, but rather allow it to be a movement of the Spirit towards us, in which it plays with us, we can be sure of an endlessly resourceful and energizing social life, the social life of prayer.[14]

Chapter Ten
ANSWERS
to PRAYER

To doubt that our prayers are answered is a modern worry, reflecting the temper of our times. But the question sounds an ancient human theme, that of wanting to reach out, to feel in relation to life around us, somehow to touch the source of all life, mysterious as it is. The doubt that anything comes back and the accompanying need for clear proof bedevil us with a sometimes terrifying insistence. We need to know. We need indisputable proof. Otherwise we feel overwhelmed by our discouragement and spiritual insecurity.

Answers do come to prayers, both clear and unclear answers. What starts as an anxious query to God — "Are you there? Do you hear me? — or a defiant demand — "Prove it to me! Show me a sign!" — turns into fear in the presence of the holy. What begins as worry that our prayers are not answered, ends, if we keep on praying, in awe that answers really do come. When that happens, we grow cautious about what we pray for.

Answers come in many forms, summed up best, perhaps, by the feeling that as a result of praying we get more self and more God. Father Boutauld stresses that God's way of speaking to us is different from our words, but "in reality He is not silent. He has a certain way of speaking which is proper to Him. . . . Imperceptibly thought will rise in your mind which will console you and calm your fears. A light will shine dispersing your doubts and uncertainties. You will be led to reflections which will show you what you have to do and indicate the surest way of succeeding in your plans. . . . He does this, not by proffering audible words but by communicating to your heart His light, His thoughts, His consolations and joys. It is His heart which speaks to His Spouses and in a language which they understand well."[1]

God answers us in the flesh of our experiences — physical, emotional, intellectual, imaginative, spiritual. Prayers change us when we are answered by an expansion of self, by more self made more accessible to us. The words with which we pray to God lead us into ourselves, to hear that primary speech so actively discoursing within ourselves. New thoughts come to mind; we see new communications between things we were thinking. New ideas of what we should be doing spring up; a new willingness to do what we are doing arises. Old duties, as regular and onerous as daily housekeeping or office tasks, seem to fall into place and become less weighty and preoccupying. Energy to improvise and imagine different courses of action and ways of seeing things comes to us.

One way prayers are answered is through this enlivening of self. We feel not only more alive and real but more our own selves. We belong to ourselves. Prayer brings excitement. We know the thrill of producing an original idea or fresh feeling, one we have come upon by ourselves and out of ourselves, not one pasted on or copied from others, not forced down our throats as "the right thing to do." We feel more connected to reality. We know what we know at firsthand on the authority of our being. The result is that reality is more immediate to us and the largeness of the immediate moment becomes more clear. Time changes for us. It no longer slips by, a waste, heavy on our hands, lost. It becomes a luxurious container for us. We have all the time we need and we have a sense of its fullness. We feel more possible in body, mind and soul. More happens to us and we take better notice of everything that happens to us and to others. So many thoughts to sort through, so many sides to problems confronting us, so many different layers of attitude and emotion! Setting out to pray to God, we have brought back a true sense of self. We feel well-fed, as if nourishment were coming to us from all directions at once. We remember moments when we have been loved and we fill up with them. We remember when we have loved and the deep satisfaction of the experience. We feel released from guilty judgments, our own against ourselves, others against us, and ours against them.

As we expand, life expands. We discover one of the main answers to praying, what is perhaps its identifying mark of protection — the fact that we are kept from burning out. So often, without prayer, our good will overruns itself and gets exhausted. Our sympathy for others extends beyond itself, runs thin, and disappears. Our suffering over the meanness of others and ourselves, the betrayals of truth, and the abject misery of so many persons comes to overwhelm us. We must turn numb to our own feelings in order to survive. What began as high ambition to achieve our resolves lies deflated like a dried-out balloon. We lose our resiliency. We know what the parable means about cleansing our house of one devil only to be possessed by seven. We wanted to be too clean, indulging a kind of pride in ourselves. Our intentions blazed brightly and used up all our fuel. Prayer keeps the fire going steadily, giving warmth consistently, even if it is less fiery than our ambitions. Prayer protects us from our pretensions to omnipotence, our inflated conviction that we can do it all, by connecting us to a larger source which really can do everything.[2]

As a result of prayer, the space of our being seems to become larger and more porous, more open and less buttressed. We pay more attention to our own reactions, which now indicate to us what to move on to next — where to seek forgiveness from someone, where to keep silent; where to offer help to someone, where not to interfere. We become more supple and able to receive the gifts given us — the flash of personal recognition by a stranger in the bus that is not seductive but benevolent; the moment's thanks from a cheerful gas station attendant; the easy collaboration of a co-worker; the complete miracle of something so funny happening that we are all shaken up into a new order by the laughter that seizes us. We become more grateful and see better how much there is to be thankful for — for the person who invented self-cleaning ovens, for the chemists who discovered penicillin and its substitutes for those allergic to it, for the tree's capacity to releaf itself after a blight of caterpillars. Prayer to this other, to otherness, to God, surprises us by setting us securely in the process of our self and our world. We enter a paradoxical state. We reach for the other and are given more of our self. We reach into our self and are given more of others.

Prayers are answered by the openings of the world as well as of the self. We are often pulled into the world by our prayer and find ourselves suddenly involved and active in it. From the stillness of prayer more action can come. Prayers are answered through events. God is incarnate in history, and in our own little history God speaks to us.[3] Thus we are amazed to discover that a co-worker who had always aroused our anxiety by his gloomy forecasts that our office would be cut back or eliminated by the higher-ups in the company now does not make us feel anxious. We do not fall into the elephant trap! This is nothing short of miraculous to us, even though to a dispassionate observer it appears merely a rational reaction and long overdue. The problem for us has been that we ourselves knew what was wrong and what rational reaction should have come from us, but we could not produce it. The more we saw the trap set by our own anxiety, the more we fell into it.

In another kind of snare, we argue the same old issue with friend or spouse and are surprised to find that we do not take the same line this time. We see a new way to feel and to think and to act and we see that it is connected to our praying. We cannot prove it, but we are persuaded that it is so. Praying thus changes our sense of causality. No longer does A inevitably lead straight to B. Now A opens into H and Q and M and P as well as pointing to B. The straight line becomes curved, parabolic, inclusive. It is open to more than one possibility.

There is a remarkable coincidence of events in our lives now.[4] We pray over an impasse, for an enemy, for a loved one. Some time later a series of events occurs that we see as directly related to our prayers. Logically, the events cannot be caused by our praying, but psychologically they impress us with their immediate connection to each other and to ourselves. We may have been feeling cut off from others, isolated, not seeing a way back into human company. We pray about it. The very day our prayer begins, an old friend from the past phones us, or another friend unexpectedly invites us for a meal. This is one way prayer is answered — through little events in our own history, our own incarnating experience of something other, striking right at our daily life. Little personal things make connections that cannot be statistically proved to rest on our interventions, but which make all the difference to us who live them.

Lest we sink into magic thinking,[5] however, where God becomes a big jukebox prayer wheel and our prayers the coins that operate the machine, we must remember that sometimes the events that answer or parallel our praying are not ones we will greet with enthusiasm. Prayers are sometimes answered by the experience of more struggle, by our being plunged into situations where we must risk more than we ever dared before. For instance, we pray over a nasty conflict with a group of people. They and the conflict become still nastier. More pressure may be put on us. Prayer does not just whisk turmoil away or instantly resolve conflict. Sometimes we are put more thoroughly right in the middle of stressful battles that force us to hold more firmly to the truth as we see it. That may be the very thing we were scared to do, just because it was bound to arouse anger and dislike in others. Or, it may be we see that we must change our position, which we can only do with ill grace, and now suddenly we have received help to get on with it. We are restored to our own good graces and to God.

The language of primary speech is often the language of grace, especially when its subject matter is the answer to prayer. The reply to our beseechings on those occasions is a flow of gifts, rarely clear as to source and not often a clear and direct response to what we have asked for. That is to say, if we have petitioned for a specific amount of money or support of some precise kind, for a particular purpose in business or love or schoolwork, we do not often get the exact sum in dollars and cents, the precise favor at work, the grade on a school assignment, or the detailed show of affection we have requested. God is not a banker or credit manager, a personnel officer or intermediary in the offices of love. The graces that come in answer to prayer come, as we have indicated, in the form of new energies, freshly stimulated memories, openings of self and the world, agreeable changes in what we thought was our disagreeably fixed nature. We may indeed receive funds, sometimes much more, sometimes much less than we asked for, new jobs for old, promotions, splendid grades, an overwhelming gathering up in love. But prayer is not a cash business; it is the world of grace, which is to say its language is the language of the spirit, and its specifications are very different from what we are accustomed to.

The language of the spirit not only breaks the causal chains in which we are so used to thinking and feeling and speaking; it is deeply and fundamentally different from the way we usually address ourselves or find ourselves addressed. Even in our most spluttery and jagged utterances, there is somewhere a logical sequence which we ourselves understand, whether or not anyone else does. That more or less orderly flow of thought or feeling, in a more or less orderly direction, is not the language of the spirit. Where our speech proceeds in sequences, the spirit moves in simultaneities. Where we demand some reasonable association of ideas, or even of emotions, looking almost always for antecedents to explain consequences, the spirit gathers everything up at once and deposits it in one massive offering to our understanding. We are, all of us, creatures of parts, used to beginnings, middles, and ends because our lives are divided that way, and our language and our way of taking in language follows the same logic of process. But the spirit is one and undivided, without parts, not chained to beginnings or middles or ends, and thus not dependent upon sequential reasoning or any other rule or requirement of the life of parts. Its being is, in the theological sense of the word, simple. Its province, its everything, is wholeness. Therefore it speaks, when it speaks, in wholenesses and of wholenesses, and that is the way we must understand it.

When the spirit speaks its wholenesses, it tells us a great deal more, perhaps, than we wanted to hear. It talks to us not only about our job problems but about the whole world of work and play and living and working with others. It deals not so much with a particular school issue as with the whole learning process, with how we know and what we know and the truths to which knowledge can bring us. When it finds us in the area of love, its own very special province, it delivers us and all our dilemmas of love into the healing wholeness of love which is its natural discourse.[6]

Answers to our prayers are always wholenesses, though we may choose out of the eagerness of our hopes or the stress of our needs to see or hear only those parts of the answers that speak directly to what we have asked for. In that way, we may get our money, our grade, our job, our gesture of love. But we have missed something, maybe what matters most, if we have contented ourselves with the obvious answer to the prayer. We may feel somewhere the increase of energy or the jog to our memory but not associate it with our prayer. We may know in some way that we are not such an emotional simpleton or hoarder of anxieties as we were before, but again not make the connection to our prayers. Sometimes, in spite of ourselves, we respond in wholeness to wholeness. We are all familiar with the kind of gratefulness that immerses being when an intense pain ceases, when the stabs of a bad headache or the disembowelments of a shattering nausea come to an end. We have all been grateful to the point of including all others who have suffered similar pain, or any pain at all, in our prayers of thanks. Even what we know is merely a temporary remission of suffering can be enough to elicit such prayer. On such an occasion, we invoke the language of the spirit; we pray for everyone; we pray for an end to suffering. What is even more remarkable in such an experience of the wholeness of the spirit, we find ourselves more able to endure the lack of wholeness which characterizes the human condition.

Our prayers are answered, then, by an enlargement of our capacity to suffer and to accept suffering as an indelible part of our lives and of the lives of others. We are thrust more into the world and we are more vulnerable to its pain. We are more alert to the life hidden beneath all the noisy distractions that try to disguise its veerings off from truth. We see that we cannot blink away anymore our lethargy, our unwillingness to see the light. We must recognize now how full of prevarications, half-truths, and endless excuses we have been, how sunk in infidelity against what is authentic and what matters, how fickle and running after quick returns and flashy badges of achievement we have been, how dull and dreary and without sustained satisfaction most of the world's life is. We feel the underlying despair and our attunement to it grows stronger so that we cannot turn it off anymore. Our resonance becomes constant, even stubborn, like the so-called "obstinate bass" line in baroque music. Through such a response to the world's unhappiness, we hear the march of demonic forces, always at hand, on the move, like the tough modern baroque figurations of Mahler's Sixth Symphony. Our suffering acquires the power to span distances, so that, for example, when we read of the cruelties of repressive or torturing governments and the savageries of people in our own society, we are not able simply to detach ourselves from the terrible facts. Nor are we so horrified that we cannot acknowledge that they are facts. We know them as facts. They seep into each of our days and we learn to live with them. Our knowing by being one with others becomes a steady flow.[7] The more we continue to pray, the less we can avoid getting our feet wet in that ocean of interconnectedness among all persons that flows from the heart of God.

Prayer also uncovers to us the suffering we ourselves cause. Our too-frequent contempt for others or lack of compassion is etched into our

consciousness. We see how easily we are threatened and close up in fear.
We know our anxiety of being, see how we run from becoming all we
are and all we might be. We see how we inflict self-amputation on our
emotions, thoughts, and actions, how we mutilate our relations with
others. Even without those dramatic revelations, continued prayer shows
us how foolish we can be, in what silly schemes we entangle ourselves,
the ridiculous plot lines that stretch on for years in our relationships with
others. Prayer unmasks those ploys as boring, time-wasting, extraneous
to our world, easily to be discarded, without fuss or fanfare.

Prayer exposes us to more suffering because it rearranges our relationship to evil. As we become more attuned to ourselves and our
world, our hearing becomes more sensitive to jarring, discordant, and
plainly wrong notes. We catch almost inaudible tones, very brief pauses,
levels of communication we would have missed before. We hear how
often and how easily people can be seduced into the wrong motifs for
their lives. We understand how rare and extraordinary the harmony of
goodness is. We come to marvel over the goodness that exists rather than
dwelling endlessly on the evil that so often prevails. Our prayers expand
to include wonder and gratitude when good actions happen or wise
enunciations of truth are heard. We see and feel how vulnerable goodness
is, in whatever forms it lives, because it is so attuned to being.

Goodness is to be in being.[8] It is life. We begin to see that in its
vulnerability goodness acquires invulnerability by building up the good,
adding more substance, weight, and presence in the face of the de-
tracting, abstracting, preventing, and absenting forces of evil. Thus a
child whose feelings are hurt by classmates' ridicule astounds us with its
willingness to return to school and remain open to friendship with the
very children who were so cruel. The parents of a murdered child bring
blessings to their neighbors in their tortured journey through feelings of
hatred and revenge when they arrive at last at a healing forgiveness. A
writer living under a persecuting government astounds us by holding at
every cost to the truth of art. His wife keeps him and his work alive by
every means, goes to every extreme, even to the point of memorizing his
poems that cannot be printed, in the blind hope that someday others will
hear them. And they do, and he lives that way, in his poems of love and
faith, long after he has died in a slave camp.[9]

Prayer attunes us to scattered lights of goodness in the great darkness of our present world. We notice more and more a tiny ray here, a faint beam there, the smallest particles wherever they appear, persons individually and in small groups holding on against impossible odds to keep their obscure lights flickering.[10]

The monasteries of our times have moved out into the world. As in the earlier so-called "dark" ages when cloistered religious people provided bastions of light, culture, knowledge, and compassion — refuges in a world of barbarism — so in our time the faithful are still dispersed, each still trying to find a way to hold onto the light, to goodness, to the presence of God in the world's darkness. The church lives in a new diaspora. Prayer heartens the effort, points out the distant lights and the near lights and identifies to us others who want to build up goodness.

Goodness surprises us with its difference from what our narrow preconceptions have made of it. Our prayers are answered, for ourself and others, by events and insights that we would not earlier have called "good," sometimes by even the diametrical opposite of what we once identified as goodness. Enough experience of this kind makes us revise our question about whether or not prayer is answered. Now we ask to know what are fitting prayers for us. And then we are often startled when we look back and see how utterly wrong the results would have been had what we prayed for been granted. What a disaster that might have been! Thank God, we say now, we were not taken at our word, but instead were answered in the spirit of our prayer. Sometimes we do not see this clearly, and we bitterly hold onto our version of the good. It is so hard to reconcile ourselves in any degree to the death of a child, to a suicide, to a quixotic illness that has robbed us of our dearest love and deprived that wonderful person of life. We must pray in the dark and take more and more risks to confide everything to God, even though God confounds us.[11]

Just as prayer increases self, it also increases God's presence in our lives or our awareness of it. It is hard to tell the difference, when praying, between our awareness of God and God's presence in itself.[12] The answer to prayer is prayer — more prayer, fuller conversation, more listening, more straining to hear, more reflection on what is actually heard, on what has really happened. We must reach out to take in what we are being led to do. If we are attentive enough, we will find patterns of prayer and develop our own discipline. We will find our own way to converse with God, drawn instead of pushed, willing what we do, not forced by a sense of duty, not stuck for words or puzzled for method. The way is only the way and not the destination, only a means and never an end. Thus our praying becomes more flexible at the same time it becomes more disciplined. We develop the skill of discernment — that knack for seeing which way leads toward God, which away from God. At one period in our life, the correct procedure may simply be to sit quietly without saying any words at all. At another, reading the daily lessons of a prayer book and meditating upon them may be right. Reciting the psalms may be appropriate, or unburdening our minds to God in a rush of our own words, or simply raising the heart in a tumult of silence.

Prayer opens us into relationship with God, which is at least as particular and as varied as relationship to another person. It changes as human participants change — now angry, now intimate, now distant, now near. We go forward into God, probing the darkness, ever more in it, like a lover taking possession of his beloved. We are opened wide by God, touched within and touched all over like a lover receiving and drawing her beloved into her, like the beloved touching all he can reach. Prayers become intensely personal and at the same time more objective and formal. The prayers of the church take on meaning of a keenly subjective sort. Our own voice, particular and individual, finds it likes to join other voices speaking to God. Our primary speech opens onto the level of human speech, where others speak for us and we speak for them. Our particular history flows into human history and is clearly a part of it, distinct yet in union with others. When we pray such a prayer as "Come Thou, Holy Spirit, Restore the lives which, without Thee, are dead,"[13] we join a chorus of voices that help carry our individual voice to God. We are like Faust at the end of Goethe's epic drama, being borne upward by everyone who has ever experienced the conversion of the spirit.

Prayers are answered by our being drawn more thoroughly into the life of God. As Eckhart puts it, God is born in us. Thus the saints caution us not to start and stop the life of prayer; that can be as hazardous as starting and stopping the birth process in pregnancy. We are drawn through our particular concerns for what God may give us into God's concerns for what we may give others and give ourselves in our own otherness. We move from knowing about God to knowing God directly, much less interested in self and much more attracted to the otherness. We come even to tolerate the absence of God from our prayers. As Henry Suso points out, patient submission to God's absence is among the highest spiritual achievements: "An abandonment above all abandonment is to be abandoned in abandonment." We are drawn toward the Word, toward the love, which Simone Weil says is not consolation, but light; toward the bosom of God, as Ruysbroeck says, into the "unfathomable joy of simplicity," the "flowing-out of love," the "dark silence in which all lovers are lost."[14] We are drawn well beyond the rules of an ethic or a theology that attempts to chart God's actions and to justify suffering and disappointment by the logic of reason. We come to pray more through Jesus and the Spirit than through charted principles or proclaimed precepts. We gain more of the heritage of Christ's passion, knowing the dying and resurrection that defy our explanations yet come to be more appropriate than our efforts to understand. Like Job, we give up our single viewpoint, what Ricoeur calls our "narcissism," even though it is narcissism at its ethical highest, asking why God does not adhere to the best rules of human justice.[15] We give it all up to hear what is truly all, the whole, in order to recognize the great otherness of God that cannot be bridged from outside but only received from the other. Any answer to prayer is the right answer if we give it back to its source, to God.

We join here the ranks of those whose high degree of prayer has earned them the name of "mystics." Theirs is both a world apart and very much our own. They have been graced in special ways. They have not only been drawn toward the Word and into the bosom of the Lord; they have responded totally and moved with all their being into being itself. Nonetheless, even without full awareness of what we have been doing, all of us who enter prayer with commitment move into the paths of the "mystics" and share with them the stages of experience and understanding that lead to union.

Everyone who gets beyond the first tentative exploration of feeling in the traditional set passages of the "Our Father" knows the sharp divesting of false selves which is *purgation*. And anyone who has moved ahead in the offering of self that prepares and accompanies the gathering of fear, aggression, sexuality, and social concern into prayer knows the revelation of personal identity which is *illumination*. As for the last of the great stages, the *union* that draws us on through purgation and illumination, that, too, is a common ground for all of us, as we shall see in the last chapter. As the philosopher John McTaggart understood so well, it is "a *sine qua non* condition of love that one should be specially conscious of union with another person."[16]

It is a special consciousness that makes it possible for us to accept the majestic terms of the celebrated *Triple Way* of the mystics — purgation, illumination, and union — to describe our efforts in prayer. It is the consciousness of love. It is the grace of committed prayer. But whether or not we accept the grace and allow ourselves to revel in the love, we do feel the impact of purgation and illumination; we are inexorably drawn into Bonaventure's Triple Way.[17]

Purgation comes with a corsair's boldness into our lives when we begin to confess our fears and offer up our aggressions in prayer. When we assert, without endless hemming and hawing and turning away from the facts, the full nature of our identity, sexual and otherwise, we are well into the precincts of that purging which also goes by the name of "purification." There is a lovely irony here, for the purifying comes with the admission and acceptance of habits, attitudes, and fancies which in other generations and other practices of prayer were supposed to be shunned and stripped away, never to be known again.

Here today, in a very different world, we do not collaborate in or pride ourselves upon what earlier times might have insisted upon calling "sin," but we do scrupulously look for what identifies us to ourselves. With the aid of a larger psychological understanding, we do claim what is rightfully ours, what clearly defines us as who and what we are. We purge whatever is extraneous or hostile to that genuine self, and purge nothing so insistently or with such hardship as the denials of self which have hidden us from ourselves and cluttered up our lives. Here we say, This is what I am. No more pretension, no more denial, and no long pauses for self-abnegation and recrimination. The greatest service we perform to and for ourselves here is to stand firmly with ourselves in the purging of false coverings.

The answer to prayer that comes with purgation is dialectical.[18] We conduct a two-, three-, four-part conversation with ourselves in this purifying process. Looking at ourselves with a piercing scrutiny that cuts through layer after layer of false covering, we oppose old negations with new ones. We recognize the denials of our own reality that we have practiced again and again in the past. We see what we have sometimes known, sometimes not been aware of — the systematic denials with which we have covered up our interior existence. Now the only denial we practice is to deny denial its cruel reign over us.

Some of the unshackling that comes with prayer resembles the long, slow shedding of skins of psychoanalytic talk therapy. There, through dreams and dream analysis, association, and elaborate reconnoitering through our past and present, we remove the chains that have kept our unconscious prisoner and lost us direct access to its precious contents, good and bad. In the purgative stage of prayer, we do much of the same thing in getting at our unconscious, with a less rigorous assaying of either the contents or the means of access to them, but with the great advantage of the new consciousness that comes with this kind of prayer. We know we must, in all prayerful honesty, give up the hidden life of denial. We must admit ourselves to ourselves.

If in the purgative stage we practice the denial of denial, in the *illuminative* we learn to identify identity. The dialectic here is a stunning experience of the concrete. Where we lived through the negation of negation in purgation, we move now into a very different kind of being. The contents are human. We neither negate nor affirm; we confront and we contemplate. With our fears and aggressions and concern for others in the forefront of our being, we do not have to work so long or so hard at claiming what belongs to us. We are what we are and we are content to be. We are beginning to be content, too, that others are what they are and to accept the ambivalent textures of life as definitive for the human condition. With the understanding of suffering that has come to us at this point of development, we can live with our own pain and the pain of others. We do so, not in dreary, cowed acceptance, but with compassion and that kind of prayerful intervention that invariably compassionates and thus softens the suffering of this world. As in a major illness of the body, the symptoms and their source must be identified before any successful treatment can begin. So in the overwhelming pain that moves through the triune sufferings of body and mind and spirit, we must know what we are dealing with. We must be able and willing to face the imbalances of a world which in its complexities can never attain a simple perfection.

The identity we discover in the stage of illumination is of the kind that in the religions and asceticisms of the East has seemed to be world- and life-denying. The nirvana the Buddhists seek clearly moves against the currents of a world shackled to suffering flesh. Equally, the philosophy of religion upon which Hinduism rests can be seen to encourage a movement across the castes and through multiple reincarnations until one has retired completely from the conflicts and degradations of earthly existence. In fact, as one observes and lives with the prayer life of almost all the sects of Buddhism and Hinduism, one discovers a contemplative wisdom which rather affirms than denies this world and its life.[19] The affirmation comes through the illumination that accompanies a constant dwelling on interior truths. Whatever the ultimate meaning for Buddhists and Hindus of their activities in this life, as Brahmin or warrior or peasant, in their prayers they look for the same centering of being that we all do. What makes the most gifted of them so compelling to meet and to understand, with and without words, is the clear mark of illumination they bear. They have achieved a dignity in the struggle for existence that is unmistakably written on their faces and in their bearing. The identity to which the stage of illumination is consecrated is actually visible in them.

The cultures of the West do not easily permit the adoption of Eastern practice. Only too often, when various Hindu and Buddhist cults have been domesticated in Europe or the Americas, they have turned or seemed to turn crackpot. They have found entertaining niches in television talk shows and accompanying enterprises in Hollywood, New York, Paris, London, or Rome. They have stirred up cocktail party conversation and college undergraduate enthusiasm. And they have tripped over and into some severely diseased or disease-prone environments, such as those of the drug communes, the Charles Manson sociopaths, and the like. In the West, enlightenment must come through an illumination that does not deny the seamy realities of a distorted religiosity and will not, in search of the wisdom we associate with Eastern contemplation, settle for a murderous caricature.[20]

In this pivotal stage of illumination, we find our identity in the enlargement of our willingness to be ourselves that we discovered in the purgative experience. We put on no new costumes to replace the old coverings. We adopt no shiny rhetorics to efface the ones which have let us down or permitted us not to know or admit to being ourselves. There is no plastic surgery in the life of the spirit, least of all in the stage of illumination. Here what is new and sparkling in its freshness is in the realm of interiority and not for a very long time to be found on the surface. If wisdom is ever made visible in us, it is not by conscious donning of mien or moue. It comes from within. It finds its own way into the outside world, and we may be the last to recognize it in ourselves, if we ever see it at all. And yet we know it, or at least what really matters in knowing it. We know that inner peace which is the identity of illumination. We pray with a movement of the heart, a lifting of the spirit. There are no convulsions, no wild urges, even interiorly. We know the light and we pray the light. We have received the most considerable answer to our prayers: more prayer.

That is where union begins. We go through words to get beyond words. Infused with prayerful understanding, we need no longer struggle with any of the grammars or syntaxes of the body, verbal or physical, to reach the spirit. The spirit has reached us.

Chapter Eleven
THE END: TRANSFIGURATION

There is no one right way to pray. The more we pray and the more we learn about the way others pray, the more sure we become about this. Different approaches abound to provide room for each of us to explore, improvise, and find his or her own way in prayer. They support us as we begin to take hold of the astounding truth that God loves us in the flesh, that our reality *is* reality. Our particular way is prized, whether through desire or despair, aggression or tranquility, groping clumsily for understanding or going straight to our goal. Our experience in prayer tells us that God wants us and accepts us as we are. What is not wanted is outward compliance with the rules while inwardly we chafe in rebellion and grievance. No deals. No bargaining. No saying that if we yield here, then God must yield there. No righteous puffing up over how splendidly we keep the rules. No guaranteed rewards. Our prayers tell us in every possible way that God wants a desiring heart, a glad heart, an angry heart, a fearful heart — our heart just as it is, freely given and fully exposed.[1]

The many different kinds of holy men and women, the lovers of God, each so different in temperament and psychological type, embolden us to believe that each of us can find our own way. For some, Ruysbroeck appears to be showing a way that is like a convulsive drowning in prayer, where we must be engulfed in great seas of feeling and utterly lost to consciousness. To others, Bernard of Clairvaux, for all his magnificence, appears to be cutting off all expression of sexuality and aggression from the spiritual life except in projected and exaggerated form, lavishing questionable emotion on the Virgin, indulging in savage attacks against the "heathen." John of the Cross looks to some to be too ascetic, too full of harsh mortification. Beatrice of Nazareth is another who is too emotional. Meister Eckhart is too full of self, too concerned with his own odd configurations of thought. Simone Weil is too much identified with the plight of the worker. Boehme is too caught up in occult oddnesses. Merton is too much involved with the politics of war and Zen Buddhism.

Whatever the differences among them, they all show that prayer is exposure, that prayer changes us, that it leads somewhere specific and is not just an aimless wandering with no discernible purpose in mind. Its purpose is exposure to everything that is in us and the willingness to receive the inevitable changes that come as a result. "Transfiguration" is the awesome word that best describes the changes.

In its most obvious meaning, transfiguration represents a change in appearance. Our shape is altered, our outer form is made different. In Scripture, the change is specific: Jesus is made glorious in transfiguration. He shines with a heavenly brightness as he talks with Moses and Elijah on the mountain. From a cloud God's voice declares Jesus's sonship as Christ and asserts the authority that goes with it. The glory of this transformation is made immediately present. The role of Jesus is no longer conveyed simply through wondrous deeds. While still in this earthly life the Lord appears in his glory, manifesting the kingdom of God on earth. Jesus is shown in the company of Old Testament heroes, to say in effect that the law is fulfilled in him. In the same way his conversation, recorded in Luke, looks forward to the great events of his passion, death, and resurrection at Jerusalem as means to work our redemption from sin, fulfilling the promise of the Exodus begun in Egypt so long ago.[2]

Prayer is taking the risk of exposing ourselves to an ultimate change of this dimension. We are called to transfiguration even though we seem an eternity from its accomplishment and the terms of its accomplishment in us must be proportionately smaller than those of the life of Jesus, in keeping with our finite dimensions.[3] But for us, anything approaching such a change would be momentous, even if our experiences of it were so gradual that it was all but imperceptible except when looked back upon from the viewpoint of eternity. The promise, not only of Scripture, but of the primary speech to which we have been giving our earnest attention, is being fulfilled:"Knock and it shall be opened unto you. Seek and you shall find. Ask and it shall be given." Something does come in; entrance is made. We remember the words: "Behold, I stand at the door and knock; [whoever] opens the door, I will come in to him and eat with him."[4] The entry is of otherness.

In praying we risk major changes by taking what seem endless small steps toward the end purpose of life. We move toward that glory in which all the words that glorify the Lord and sing God's praises seem understatements. It is as if the wide and varied fabric of our prayers had been grasped at the center and pulled inside out to reveal everything in a blaze of understanding. The fabric remains the same — we are not called out of our fleshly existence. But what was hidden is now shown to us; what was far below us in shrouded darkness is now right before us in the light. The way things appear to us and the way we appear to others have both been fundamentally changed.

We have reached the last of the stages of the Triple Way, *union*. Our lives have been transfigured through prayer. This sounds momentous, as it should. But it is not so rare as all that. We need not begin to think of ourselves as keeping company with the mystics and start looking for the more startling signs of what is usually called "infused prayer" — a little levitation, a bit of bi-location, a passing vision or two.[5] Those things make up the show business aspects of the world of prayer and come more in the lurid accounts of those who are, in effect, the groupies surrounding holy men and women than in the actual experience of those gifted people. The unitive way of prayer that follows the purgative and illuminative is the way of new understanding, direct understanding, truth revealed by sudden accession of understanding. This way has such unmistakable grace, in both senses of the word, as a gift from God and as an effortless and marvelously finished comprehension, that it seems altogether otherworldly. It is not hard to call what we take in in this way a "vision." It so transcends ordinary ways of thinking, feeling, and learning that it cannot help but be associated with the bizarre feats of the "surprising" mystics.[6] Nonetheless, it is a way of seeing, hearing, and feeling, of tasting and touching, of knowing, in sum, that comes to all who persevere in prayer and bring themselves, through the scouring away of pretension and denial that is purgation and the affirmation of human identity that is illumination, to the transfiguring effects of union.

The unitive way is the most intimate and private of the three stages of the Triple Way. Though the effects of our transfiguration will, in time, show not only in our behavior but in our looks, we do not have a ready subject here for general discussion or sharing with others, even those we love who are most close to us. Even in a time when there is nothing that occurs in sexual intimacy that someone will not bring up somewhere for discussion and, if necessary, for demonstration before a motion picture camera, the highly private stage of unitive prayer does not make its way comfortably into public discussion. Union means what its name suggests. We are made one with otherness in some incalculably direct way that we know we have experienced. We prepare for it as we do for the most precious intimacies. We move with delicacy, with endless care for what is so unmistakably otherly to us. The care becomes an even more fragile awe when we discover in the otherness glimmers and touches of ourselves, mirrorings of our existence which reflect us and in their reflection of us point all the more to their differences from us. We alternate movement with stillness, words with silence. We contemplate. With or without instruction, we know there are times in this most elegant and transfixing of experiences when we must simply wait, wait to catch up with the rhythm, wait to be caught up with, wait to know and to be known.

The Spanish mystics are particularly gifted with the words to describe the unitive way. Teresa of Avila's *Interior Castle* concludes in a blaze of crystalline light in which the union of creature and Creator is all but palpable. In her meditation on the Song of Songs, she speaks of the way the soul feels the presence of God in all its faculties, in a "sweetness" in which the whole person, "inward and outward, is strengthened and comforted, as if a most sweet ointment were poured into the very marrow of the soul. . . . Nor do we know what it is nor whence that fragrance comes, but it pervades us through and through." She strains the physical facts of sexuality to make her joyous point, endowing the God-man with the transcendent beauty of the woman of the Song: "It seems to the soul that she is held up in those divine arms and fastened to that sacred side and those divine breasts, and she can do nothing but rejoice, sustained with the divine milk with which her Bridegroom is nourishing her. . . ."[7]

In the rhythms of the unitive stage, we find ourselves anew. We discover that, turned inside out as we have been, we are actually closer to what we are meant to be than we ever were before when we were right side up. What we are going through is a process of exposure of ourselves to ourselves, in which the Bride is the Bridegroom and the Bridegroom is both himself and his spouse, in which to receive is to give and to give is to receive, for both are functions of attention. We are attentive now to being, our own and others'. We are attentive to being itself. We understand, in the direct way of union, that it is only in the attention we give to otherness that we find our own being. We know that not even the most daring claim we have ever made or could make for ourselves, the most demanding cry for attention, the most insistent drawing of a person or an experience to ourselves for our own gratification, can begin to match the personal satisfaction that comes from this going out to otherness. This total giving is, finally, a complete receiving. To understand that fact in the immediacy of experience is to be utterly changed, to be transfigured. To see all of ourselves from such a vantage point is an exposure of being unlike any other, for which the only appropriate name is transfiguration.

The exposure and change occur very gradually, as parts of a long-range process. In early prayer we begin to discover our names for God, the names by which we address ultimate otherness in conversation. As we go on praying, we uncover the names for our relation to God and the images we have projected onto God through which God reaches us. We have found a place in our images and projections like Jacob's, on an ascending and descending ladder.[8] It is a ladder that does not reach all the way to the top or descend all the way to the depths, and yet it has an end. Our images of God cannot be translated into the reality of God. Prayer will be and must be overtaken by silence. A gap must exist between our self and this other. Unknowing, we wait. Learning of a new God-given language that may not have any words in it, we are convinced that the gap will be spanned from the other's side. Attempting to close the gap entirely from our side, we would lose ourselves altogether in the gap. We do not find God simply by our efforts. Here, we recover ourself; we receive God's name for us. We come to see how we are seen, how the sheep and goats in us are recognized and separated. We are the sinners; still, we are brought into the loving embrace. We come to see how our subjective self is the object of a greater subject's attention.[9]

Ruysbroeck writes movingly of this great event of name-giving, signified by the Christ-experience. In the Father's fathomless darkness, the Son shines as a single ray of brightness illuminating our inward being and our reason. The Son is the connection between us and God. Jesus is what Ruysbroeck calls the "sparkling stone." It is an image like the priceless pearl of the New Testament and the alchemical "lapis" that Jung used to signify the self, the very center of the human psyche that connects it to a transpersonal reality beyond it.[10] In this stone is the ray of ever-lasting light, a beam of God's glory, a flawless mirror in which all things can live. Like a flame of fire, it gives us light and life, filling the whole kingdom of being with everlasting love. The sparkling stone is the gift of grace to the lovers of God. In it is hidden a new name for the soul which no one knows but the one who receives it. This is the name by which God addresses us in Christ, the name conferring on us an identity of eternal value.

How do we experience this and know that we do? With paradox. The self, so securely named, so fully given, fills us with solid identity, so much self. Yet it is a self ultimately derived, utterly dependent, and even named from a source outside itself. Such riches because of such poverty — such fullness because of such emptiness. All that we would hold most dear and protect most earnestly is transmuted into our own bits of gold and frankincense and myrrh to bring to the child in us and the child outside us.

We have again that sense of our prayers being answered where we feel drawn more and more irresistibly into God's life, so that at points it is sometimes as if God were actually praying through us and in us. We exist as vessel, as conduit, as an arrow drawn from another's bow. The feeling of living a borrowed life intensifies. We want to offer more.

When we open to that knock on the door and go on opening, we feel the entering of God in all the new little events of our life. We know the beginnings of new being as thoughts, possible actions, attitudes, in-creased sorrow over our foolishness, increased joy over our love. All these arouse in us a wish to give and then to give more. We want to spread out on the table whatever we have in our house to offer. We are led, we are driven. We move quickly, we move slowly to find those central themes in our lives around which our lives have revolved, those lines on which our sense of self has been strung out like so much wash.

Those basic themes of attitude and personality come to be what we want to offer, what we experience as the essence of what we are, the defining myths by which we have lived. These we want to offer to our entering guest. Thus we enter the mysterious realm of transfiguration where we give into God's hands what have been our most defining human themes, and receive God's defining action for ourselves.

These themes come to be quite familiar to us, though we are a long time recognizing them. Sometimes it takes a whole lifetime, and only at the moment of death do we find we can offer them into God's hands. Sometimes, we know parts of the themes, seeing them clearly at crisis points in our lives, only to lose them when we recover our daily routine. Illness, loss, suffering are times when we are apt to discover these themes. Steady prayer over the years brings them to our awareness with a clarity that can be blinding.

We may see how our whole life has been dominated by one color alone — being our father's son or mother's daughter, for example. We have never cut ourselves entirely free from parental support, but have hung on to a supported life out of fear we could not stand on our own. As a result, we now see, we have lost our life; we lack self-esteem or even gratefulness for the support of our parent. We revile father or mother or both for failing us. This angry dependence and this abysmal fear of failing emerge as the central theme in our sense of self. This we bring; this we offer.

We may now see how our whole life is dominated by a myth of victimhood, a myth we unconsciously helped to make true in repeated events, for it validated our need for such an identity. Despite our outcry that all these mishaps occurred to us, we may come to see how much we in fact made them happen. And so now it is this victimhood that will comprise our offering.

We may come to see that our whole life has been a struggle to champion the underdog and to fight injustice. Concealed in that myth will be truth and falsity. We, in our furious fighting, have brought up the tanks, the great pressures against our opponents, in precisely the same style of oppression we have so long attacked in others. We have fattened off this self-image as a fighter against injustice, and it is this we want now to give up in our offering.

We may recognize the theme of power in our lives, the need to be first always, to win all the games, to be successful, rich, and influential. We may see how this urge, this need, has dominated our existence and that it is the most precious possession we have to bring. We may see that our need for praise and constant good opinion is the major theme of our work and relationships, that above all else we wanted to keep hidden our faults and vices. Under threat of mental illness or dying we may fear that these buried facts will rise to claim us and that we will be unmasked. This deep fear, this managing of our own reputation, this supervision of our dignity, will then comprise our offering. We may see that those we love or have loved and who have loved us form the great content of our lives. Then that is what we must bring to cover the table for our guest.

The formal prayer of oblation in a Eucharist service quickens into life: "We offer our selves, our souls, our bodies and minds to be a reasonable and living sacrifice. . . . "[11] We may come to want to offer our life itself into God's hands, the whole thing, in toto. This happens to people when they are close to death and it can happen to people when they still feel far from death. The whole cloth is bundled into God's hands.

God does not want the sacrifice that leads to death but living devotion, the sacrifice that leads to life, so that we give up into his hands all that identifies us, all the extremes of our being, our best and our worst. We offer our best love, our worst fear, our best wishes and hopes, our worst despair, our best values and our most corrupt, everything by which we have striven to live. We die to our own small versions of reality; we give into God's care our mythical gods and the gods of our personal and collective myths. These are the gifts we bring to our epiphany.

This means we are living now in rearranged form. We are the same persons and yet radically different. The difference is hidden from view except for us who experience it. It is also a difference hidden from acclaim, hidden in the closet of prayer, never to be brought out and displayed in public.

A new theme takes root at the center of our lives, and all time and space are reordered for us. It is a move in time of the consequence of the shift from B.C. to A.D. The theme that dominates our lives now is the effort to correspond with grace. We want to go with the little signs and fragments of new being given us in prayer; we want to be alert to their coming in the world. We want to traffic in this commodity; we want to agree with its impetus, to speak back and forth with it. All else comes to orbit around the giving of grace, the large signs of it in history and the major events of our lives that all can see and the small signs discernible only to those of us who experience it. We may still value what we valued before this wish to offer everything took shape, but we feel our feeling in a different space, the space of absolute beginnings.[12] Those values that survive this profound alteration, this setting off from a new departure point, thrive and increase, as for example in our love for child and spouse. God comes to bring life, and abundantly, not to make small and meager. We risk ourselves in these loves, even more daringly than before as we relinquish our managerial rights over them, folding them into God's embrace. God gathers us like a goose taking her goslings under her wide strong wings.

Such a love of others in God grows tough and moves away from sentimentality. Sentimentality only masquerades as love; it is really only an uneasy joining together of power and fear. Under a brittle shell of control of the other, one is so mushily afraid of what will happen to oneself if something unpleasant should happen to the other. This new love grows sure and firm and finds conviction and hope in looking at the other and looking out for the other. One is free to take risks on behalf of the other. We can risk, for example, getting angry at a child, no longer held back by fear the child will withdraw its love. One's love goes out to the child for the child's sake, not to gain good opinion for oneself. Such a love endures, surviving disappointments. Such a love insists on expanding, itself becoming the center of a life. One principal sign of grace that has been corresponded to is a life lived more and more out of a central and centering love. There are many signs. This is the abundance God has promised us. Lady Julian of Norwich says "Love is the Lord's meaning. . . . " A parallel wisdom is in the dictum that "Only what has turned to love in your life will be preserved."[13] That is the promised abundance.

The signs of abundance that come with this love deposit eternity in our laps. We can feel permanence, positively taste it, as perhaps we have before in the throes of puppy love or in marriage or even in short-lived, intense love affairs. The difference now is that the recipient, the source of our love, is not reducible to the moods and fancies, the vagaries or the temperamental uncertainties of another human person. There are no losses to an insecure psyche, no tremors in the face of a badly assimilated aggression. We do not worry whether he really means these honeyed words or is simply indulging our need for constant reassurance. We do not have to suppress our strong feeling or the physical expression that accompanies it for fear she will be frightened by such a torrent of love.

There are instead all the delights of relationship we have ever known or hoped for and something more besides — the conviction, based on experience, that it will last. Everything else, everyone else we love is part of this love, too. The Lord our God may be, in the language of the Old Testament, a jealous God, but not jealous in this way. All love that is love, that is not merely a tickling and an appeasement of an appetite, is welcome in the love of God. And all love endures alongside and within this love, for the presence that witnesses and secures this love offers its fullness and understanding in support and extension of everything we have known or can know of love.

Language falters in the attempt to explain the love of the unitive stage. Language is necessarily complex. It is always moving from expressed meaning to unexpressed, from denotation to connotation. In the way we usually talk to each other and to ourselves, we search for resonances, for layers and layers of meaning that will perhaps bring us eventually to truth or some part of truth. But as all of us know who have done the kind of thinking that is closely tied to feeling, words and phrases do not say it all for us. There are underlying thought-feelings, or feeling-thoughts for which there simply are no verbal or syntactical equivalents. We must go beyond words, confiding ourselves to God, letting God help us lift our hearts to him in silence and sometimes even without images.

All of this is particularly clear to us when we reach the upper terraces of prayer. At the transfiguring height of union, we are well beyond words, yet not outside either thought or feeling. We try, if only to sort out some of the wonders of this moment for ourselves, to translate it into something we can hold onto, rather like a list or a quick comment on the side of a passage in a book that has caught something of importance for us, or some other mnemonic that will make the ineffable hold still. Like the mystics who turn to the images of the Song of Songs, we frequently find that narrative of wooing and sexual union satisfactory. We understand again why it must stand where it does in the Biblical canon.[14] And yet even its exalted measures may be too much, too complicated, too multifaceted and overladen with too many movements away from the central fact: love.

A life grows simple in this love, for life has been granted its principal priority. The infinite complexities of life find their sustaining structure in the grace of love. Our space is aligned to this central axis — where we live, how we live, the way we feel our interior expanses. Our sense of time is recovered. Whatever our way of praying has evolved to be, we see now that it comprises the major work of our day, its primary means of punctuation. All the other things we do and must do merely accompany this main theme. Prayer is dominant, our principal employment. The work of prayer goes with us everywhere. Prayer is present in the most mundane activities, sometimes so specific in its immediacy and claim on our attention that we stop whatever we are doing, at other times so much a persistent background atmosphere that it pervades whatever we are doing. Most important, the whole issue of finding time to pray just washes away. We achieve something of what Anthony Bloom calls the holiday spirit of prayer, a sense of celebration in which schedules and time-slots simply fade away.[15] We feel we have all the time in the world. In fact, we are still working and keeping appointments, doing what we have to do, but the time is different now. It is free. Nothing is fixed and ultimate because every moment receives its ultimate fixedness from God.

When we correspond with grace, we work with our image of God to bring all that we are to completion. The straight line of our life from birth to death begins to curve around this center, stretching it into that famous circle that has its center everywhere and its circumference nowhere, the circle that links everything to the whole.[16] The great devotees of prayer use dramatic images to speak of this process, a process often characterized for them by a very dramatic feeling of surrender. The dying to self and rising in the Lord is the point of that surrender. Such deep and wise reordering of our little being opens us to the largeness of being in new ways.

Ricoeur says we move toward a God no longer sought for protection or consolation but for the display of being, a being to whom we no longer address questions of justification or requests of any kind. Rather we simply behold. What we behold is that being reaches toward us in a self-display that creates dialogue. We understand being as a speaking being, gathering all things together and establishing human being as the one that inquires about being. Our language, like a small edition of a true poetry, shows that being forth. [17] We change then from separated creatures trying to repudiate their dependency or striving to secure their dependency into persons who want to link up with the whole. We become like a little child that expresses itself coming into being in relation to others in the play, for example, or linking the cars of a toy train together. [18] We change from creatures trying to produce connections with others into persons who see that the originating connection is already there, given, to be seen, to be accepted. Thus we are joined together into what gathers everything together. We experience the primary speech of our worship in its most enabling mood, where we are permitted to behold and then to tell ourselves and others what is there, because it really is there.

Sometimes we find the images of this speech in a dream. One man whose beholding was clear dreamed of a monastery in an unusually beautiful wilderness of forests and lakes. It reminded him freshly of what had first called him to a religious attitude. Those ancient monasteries, the ruins of which he had seen on a trip abroad, spoke to him of the power of religious faith. The faith seemed to emanate from those who possessed it like bees buzzing from a hive with a remarkable fullness of activity and presence. The monastery with its rounds of chants and prayers is witness to some objective presence; it is there, whether we know it or not. The constant prayers of the faithful exist in unceasing connection with the presence. Such an image, such a memory, such an original attraction speaks of the possibility of being related to this source, a bidding not easily ignored.

St. Teresa of Avila talks of the garden watered by God's rain, John of the Cross of the infusion of love into the soul, Richard Rolle of a "sweet and delectable light" and the "mirth of love." Bernard writes of the fire of God's love deepening the iron of the soul into something stronger and hotter, making it as a result both more itself and more God's. [19]

The prayer we begin for our own sake comes finally to be offered for God's sake. Elizabeth of the Trinity writes of the "consuming fire" which extends all over the members of Christ's mystical body, saying "Then we shall console the Heart of Jesus . . . and he will be able to say, showing us the Father: 'Now I am glorified in them. . . . ' ' '[20] In saying anything like that, we are saying a great deal. We are asserting a closeness to God so great that we presume to comfort his son. We also are assuming so considerable a rise in our experience of God that we can talk of making our offerings, offering our prayers, praying our lives for God's sake and not our own, a stage of understanding and grace that for the medieval mind would have been all but impossible to reach here on earth.[21]

Transfiguration does bring with it a holy audacity. We dare almost anything because almost everything seems to have been placed within our grasp. We feel ourselves taken up, questioned, held, and answered by being itself. What movement of the heart, no matter how brazen, can match the extravagance of that fancy? And what if it is true? What lover who has experienced union can deny being transformed, even if only for seconds at a time?

If we have made our way in prayer to this height, we are not likely to spend much time in the dismal processes of self-questioning, looking for all the ways in which we can be found unworthy. Of course we are unworthy in any absolute sense. That is a settled issue. As spiritual writers have remarked before, all we need to do is think who God is and who we are to see with blinding precision just how unworthy we are. But the fact remains that, for the believer who becomes the full-fledged experiencer, that same God who is so far beyond us is also right here within us. By that God we were made, moved, enlarged, and woven into ultimate being. By that God we were joined.

It is the joining that we know at the top of our experience. It is to the joining that the experiences of so many others give full testimony. It is the joining that an incomparable literature tells us about, from the first moments that words are shaped in history, or pictures painted, or music composed, to speak about human interiority. In the joining, we join ourselves; we meet all who have come before, all who are here with us, all who will ever be, all who in any way are a part of that joining. We are finite; we began our lives, as best we can understand them, at a point in time. But we know ourselves now to have gone through time to touch something that is outside time. We are experiencing transfiguration in another dimension — we go past figuration, past words or images, past numbers or lines, past sounds, sights, tastes, touches, and smells. We go from being apart to joining, and we find ourselves all the more ourselves in the joining. We know, finally, how utterly wordless primary speech must be when it becomes the Word.

Appendix
THE ART
of PRAYER

By the art of prayer, we mean those works of art that for one reason or another have proved useful in prayer. Some of these works seem to come from prayer. Others lead directly to prayer. Some have an open and clear religious content. Others seem as far removed from the usual materials of prayer as they can be. But all those we call to your attention here are very much to the point of prayer as we have discussed it in this book. They touch the imagination, lift it, and free it to perform its primordial task of reconciling us to being.

We have limited ourselves here to composers, poets, painters and sculptors and have kept the number reasonably small. All the music listed is available on record and seems likely to remain so. The paintings and sculpture are obviously best seen "in the flesh," so to speak, in their original form, in museums or galleries. But that is not always possible and so we have been careful to choose painters and sculptors whose works are well reproduced in those books and postcards and slides that André Malraux called "museums without walls" and are easily accessible. The same principle has urged the choice of poets whose work is all around us, in libraries and in a variety of hardbound and paperback editions.

COMPOSERS

Johann Sebastian Bach:

There are of course a vast number of works with explicit religious content or concern by Bach — the Cantatas, the Chorale Preludes, the Motets, etc.— and a whole world of keyboard, orchestral, and chamber music. We particularly recommend the *St. Matthew Passion*, the *St. John Passion*, the *Magnificat*, the *Christmas Oratorio*, the *Easter Oratorio*, *The Musical Offering*, and the *Chromatic Fantasy and Fugue in D Minor*.

Samuel Barber:
Prayers of Kierkegaard.

Bela Bartók:
The String Quartets.

Ludwig van Beethoven:
Some adventuring among the Piano Sonatas and the Violin and Piano Sonatas, the late String Quartets (nos. 12 to 16 and the *Grosse Fuge*), the Fourth Piano Concerto, and the *Missa Solemnis.*

Alban Berg:
String Quartet.

Hector Berlioz:
L'Enfance du Christ.

Ernst Bloch:
Sacred Service (*"Avodath Hakodesh"*).

Johannes Brahms:
The Piano Quartets and Quintet, the Violin and Piano Sonatas, the Trios, *Four Serious Songs*, and the *German Requiem.*

Anton Bruckner:
Mass No. 2 in E minor, the *Te Deum*, and the Ninth Symphony.

Ferrucio Busoni:
The Piano Sonatinas.

Marc-Antoine Charpentier:
The Masses.

Frederic Chopin:
The Etudes, the Preludes, and the Scherzos.

George Crumb:
Ancient Voices of Children.

Luigi Dallapiccola:
Il Prigioniero.

Claude Debussy:
The piano music, the String Quartet.

Frederick Delius:
Requiem.

Ernst Von Dohnanyi:
Variations on a Nursery Song.

Guillaume Dufay:
Any of the Masses.

Antonin Dvořák:
Mass in D Major, the Trios, the Piano Quartets.

Edward Elgar:
The Dream of Gerontius, the *Enigma Variations*.

Duke Ellington:
Sacred Concerts, *Black, Brown and Beige*.

Gabriel Fauré:
Requiem.

César Franck:
The organ music.

Christoph Willibald Glück:
Orfeo ed Euridice.

Gregorian Chant

George Frederick Handel:
The Messiah, Israel in Egypt, the Organ Concertos.

Franz Josef Haydn:
The Masses (even the least of them), adventuring through the Piano Sonatas, Piano Trios, String Quartets, and Symphonies — a large number, and worth the prayerful effort.

Paul Hindemith:
Mathis der Maler, The Four Temperaments.

Arthur Honegger:
Symphony No. 3 (*"Liturgique"*).

Charles Ives:
Concord Sonata, Symphony No. 4.

Leos Janacek:
Sonata for Violin and Piano, the *Glagolitic Mass*.

Franz Liszt:
Années de pèlerinage (for piano).

Guillaume de Machaut:
Notre Dame Mass.

Gustav Mahler:
Das Lied von der Erde, Sixth and Ninth Symphonies.

Frank Martin:
The Concertos.

Felix Mendelssohn:
The Octet, the Sextet, the Quartets.

Olivier Messiaen:
La Nativité du Seigneur (for organ), *Quartet for the End of Time, Visions de l'amen* (for piano).

Claudio Monteverdi:
Madrigals, *Vespers*.

Wolfgang Amadeus Mozart:
The choice, as with Bach and Haydn, is endless. We recommend the *Ave Verum Corpus*, the so-called *Great C Minor Mass*, the *Requiem*, the opera *The Magic Flute*, the Violin and Piano Sonatas, the Piano Quartets, and the *Sinfonia Concertante in E Major* (for violin and viola), adventuring among the Piano Concertos, Piano Sonatas, and Symphonies.

Modest Mussorgsky:
Songs and Dances of Death.

Giovanni Palestrina:
The Song of Songs.

Krzysztof Penderecki:
Dies Irae (Auschwitz Oratorio).

Françis Poulenc:
The opera *Dialogues of the Carmelites*.

Sergei Prokofiev:
Third Piano Concerto, First Violin Concerto, Piano Sonatas 2, 7, 8, and 9.

Sergei Rachmaninoff:
Vespers, adventuring among the songs and piano music.

Maurice Ravel:
Gaspard de la Nuit (for piano), the Trio.

Gioacchino Rossini:
Stabat Mater.

Domenico Scarlatti:
The Sonatas (for either harpsichord or piano).

Arnold Schoenberg:
The opera *Moses and Aaron*, the String Quartets.

Franz Schubert:
Piano Sonatas in A Major (D. 959) and B Flat (D. 960), the Quintets, the song cycle *Die Winterreise*, the Trios, Quartets, and Symphonies.

Robert Schumann:
The Piano Quartet and Piano Quintet, *Carnaval* (for piano), the song cycle *Dichterliebe* and *Frauenliebe und -leben*.

Heinrich Schütz:
Easter Oratorio, Motets.

Alexander Scriabin:
The Piano Sonatas.

Dmitri Shostakovitch:
Symphonies 14 and 15, Sonata for Viola and Piano, the song cycles setting poems by Tsvetayeva and Michelangelo, adventuring among the String Quartets.

Jean Sibelius:
Fourth and Sixth Symphonies.

Richard Strauss:
Death and Transfiguration, Four Last Songs.

Igor Stravinsky:
Symphony of Psalms, Mass.

Peter Ilyitch Tchaikovsky:
The opera *Eugen Onegin, Souvenir de Florence* (string sextet).

Edgar Varese:
Ionisation, Poème Electronique.

Ralph Vaughan Williams:
Flos Campi, Dona Nobis Pacem.

Guiseppe Verdi:
Requiem, the opera *Otello*.

Tomas Luis de Victoria:
O Magnum Mysterium.

Antonio Vivaldi:
Gloria in D Major.

Richard Wagner:
  Siegried Idyll, Wesendonck Songs, the opera *Parsifal*.

Anton Webern:
  Pieces for String Quartet.

Hugo Wolf:
  Mörike Lieder.

POETS

Anna Akhmatova
Angelus Silesius
W. H. Auden
Charles Baudelaire
John Betjeman
William Blake
Boethius
Paul Celan
Geoffrey Chaucer
John Clare
Paul Claudel
Samuel Taylor Coleridge
William Cowper
Hart Crane
Richard Crashaw
e. e. cummings
Dante Alighieri
Sir John Davies
Emily Dickinson
John Donne
John Dryden
William Dunbar
T. S. Eliot
Robert Frost
Johann Wolfgang Goethe
Thomas Hardy
George Herbert
Heinrich Hölderlin
Gerard Manley Hopkins
Solomon Ibn Gabirol
Max Jacob

Elizabeth Jennings
John of the Cross
Samuel Johnson
David Jones
John Keats
Gertrud Kolmar
William Langland
Louis MacNeice
Stéphane Mallarmé
Osip Mandelstam
Marie de France
Andrew Marvell
Czeslaw Milosz
Edwin Muir
Ovid
Boris Pasternak
Charles Péguy
Francesco Petrarca
Alexander Pope
Ezra Pound
Alexander Pushkin
Rainer Maria Rilke
Arthur Rimbaud
William Shakespeare
Vladimir Solovyev
Edmund Spenser
Wallace Stevens
Allen Tate
Dylan Thomas
R. S. Thomas
Thomas Traherne

Marina Tsvetayeva
Paul Valéry
Henry Vaughan
François Villon

Virgil
William Wordsworth
W. B. Yeats

PAINTERS AND SCULPTORS

Josef Albers
Fra Angelico
Hans Arp
Gian Lorenzo Bernini
Pierre Bonnard
Sandro Botticelli
Constantin Brancusi
Georges Braque
Pieter Breughel the Elder
Massimo Campigli
Michelangelo Caravaggio
Mary Cassatt
Paul Cézanne
John Constable
Lucas Cranach the Elder
Carlo Crivelli
Gerard David
Edgar Degas
Donatello
Albrecht Dürer
Max Ernst
Jan van Eyck
Jean Fouquet
Helen Frankenthaler
Naum Gabo
Paul Gauguin
Lorenzo Ghiberti
Giorgione
Giotto di Bondone
Vincent van Gogh
El Greco
Arshile Gorky
Adolph Gottlieb
Morris Graves

Matthias Grünewald
Hans Holbein the Younger
Pieter de Hooch
Vassily Kandinsky
Paul Klee
Franz Kline
Oskar Kokoschka
Käthe Kollwitz
Willem de Kooning
Georges de La Tour
Leonardo da Vinci
René Magritte
Aristide Maillol
Alfred Manessier
Andrea Mantegna
John Marin
Masaccio
Henri Matisse
Hans Memling
Michelangelo
Piet Mondrian
Claude Monet
Berthe Morisot
Henry Moore
Louise Nevelson
Barnett Newman
Ben Nicholson
Emil Nolde
Parmigianino
Pablo Picasso
Piero della Francesca
Pinturicchio
Serge Poliakoff
Jackson Pollock

Nicholas Poussin
Ad Reinhardt
Rembrandt van Rijn
Auguste Renoir
Jusepe de Ribera
Tilman Riemenschneider
Auguste Rodin
Mark Rothko
Georges Rouault
Peter Paul Rubens

Georges Seurat
Nicholas de Staël
Tintoretto
Titian
J. M. W. Turner
Paolo Uccello
Victor Vasarély
Diego de Velazquez
Jan Vermeer
Roger van der Weyden

Notes

CHAPTER ONE

1. "Crying to God is not done with the physical voice, but with the heart; many are noisy with their mouths but with their hearts averted are able to obtain nothing. If, then, you cry to God, cry out inwardly where he hears you." On Ps. 30:3-10; cited in Thomas A. Hand, O.S.A., *Saint Augustine On Prayer* (Westminster: Newman Press, 1963), p. 70. Father Hand points out that for Augustine "heart" signifies "our whole interior and spiritual life, and it includes mind and will, knowledge and love." *Ibid.*, p. 71.

2. "Collecting" and "recollecting" are not used here in the way that they are in the technical language of the methodology of prayer, to mean particular gatherings of prayers into one *collect*, or that kind or concentration on the divine presence that makes some spiritual writers think of *recollection* as a special grace not granted to everyone. Some of the resonances of both usages are intended, however, and especially that nurturing of understanding of ourselves that we want to collect and recollect, to think back upon and keep alive. Francis de Sales describes the feeling superbly, speaking of the way one holds onto the "profitable" effects of meditation: "Retain as long as you can the feeling and affections that you have received. When a man has received some precious liquid in a porcelain vase and carries it home, he walks gently. He does not look aside but generally before him, for fear of stumbling against a stone or making a false step, and sometimes he looks upon the dish he carries, for fear of spilling the liquor. You must do the same thing when you finish your meditation. Do not let anything distract you, but

look forward with caution . . . [and] watch over your heart, so that as little of the liquor of holy prayer as possible may be spilt." St. Francis de Sales, *Introduction to the Devout Life*, trans. and ed. John K. Ryan (New York· Harper, 1950), p. 49.

3. See Ann and Barry Ulanov, *Religion and the Unconscious* (Philadelphia: Westminster, 1975), pp. 26-32.

4. Melanie Klein, the psychoanalyst noted for her work with very young children, writes, "I have often expressed my view that object-relations exist from the beginning of life, the first object being the mother's breast which to the child becomes split into a good (gratifying) and bad (frustrating) breast; this splitting results in a severance of love and hate." Melanie Klein, "Notes on Some Schizoid Mechanisms," in *Envy and Gratitude and Other Works, 1946-1963* (New York: Delacorte Press/Seymour Lawrence, 1975), p. 2.

5. "The soul, after it has been definitely converted to the service of God, is, as a rule, spiritually nurtured and caressed by God, even as is the child by its loving mother, who warms it with the heat of her bosom and nurtures it with sweet milk and soft and pleasant food, and carries it and caresses it in her arms; but as the child grows bigger, the mother gradually ceases caressing it, and, hiding her tender love, puts bitter aloes upon her sweet breasts, sets down the child from her arms and makes it walk upon its feet, so that it may lose the habits of a child and betake itself to more important and substantial occupations. The loving mother is like the grace of God. . . ." St. John of the Cross, *Dark Night of the Soul*, in *The Complete Works of St. John of the Cross*, trans. and ed. E. Allison Peers (Westminster: Newman, 1964 [1935]), p. 330. It is a figure of speech to which John is devoted. Some pages later on, for example, he speaks of the dark night as a weaning "from the breasts of these sweetnesses and pleasures. . . ." *Ibid.*, p. 349.

6. We can try to use prayer like a magical incantation to ward off frightening thoughts and feelings. We can try to use prayer to deny what depth psychologists call our narcissistic wound, to cover up to ourselves that we feel essentially alone, unlovable, and hopeless about ever-changing things. But prayer can also be a most effective means to face those very fearful thoughts and feelings, as well as a support to enable us to face our sense of being damaged at the core, at the level of our most basic self-esteem and self-acceptance. Here we use prayer to help us hear those primary voices within, instead of blotting them out. We pray a prayer of confessing, such as "Lord, I see how frightened I am about all these things," or a prayer of offering, such as, "Lord, I bring you these scary ideas of suicide; I put them into your

hands; help me with them, I almost sink beneath them; help me to put them in their proper place — neither to deny them nor to drown in them."

For a helpful discussion of narcissistic elements in religion and of the anti-narcissistic forces in religious faith, see Paul Pruyser, "Narcissism in Contemporary Religion," *The Journal of Pastoral Care*, Vol. XXXII, No. 4, December 1978, pp. 219-232.

7. Some of our examples are taken from Ann Ulanov's practice as a psychotherapist. For detailed material on persons' images of God, see Anna-Maria Rizzuto, *The Birth of the Living God* (Chicago: University of Chicago Press, 1979), chapters 6-9.

8. For an excellent summary of Husserl's theory, see John Bowker, *The Sense of God* (Oxford: Clarendon Press, 1973), pp. 173-180.

9. The transformations of the ultimate object, God, into a heightened subjectivity are more familiar to us then we can usually bring ourselves to admit. "The psychological reality is such that everyone is potentially subject to mystical experience," says Ben-Ami Scharfstein, "although, when had, it may be dismissed or called by another name . . . . Everyday mysticism expresses the power of each human self to assimilate whatever lies outside it, that is, to abolish the otherness of other persons and things." Among a number of other shrewdly chosen exhibits of "everyday mysticism," Scharfstein cites this one: "The thing happened one summer afternoon, on the school cricket field, while I was sitting on the grass, waiting my turn to bat. I was thinking about nothing in particular, merely enjoying the pleasures of midsummer idleness. Suddenly, and without warning, something invisible seemed to be drawn across the sky, transforming the world about me into a kind of tent of concentrated and enhanced significance What had been merely an outside became an inside. The objective was somehow transformed into a completely subjective fact, which was experienced as 'mine,' but on a level where the word had no meaning; for 'I' was no longer the familiar ego." Ben-Ami Scharfstein, *Mystical Experience* (Indianapolis: Bobbs-Merrill, 1973), pp. 62, 69.

10.   To seek God
means first of all
to let yourself be found by Him.
He is the God of Abraham, Isaac and Jacob.
He is the God of Jesus Christ.
He is your God,
not because He is yours
but because you are His.

> To choose God
> is to realise that you are known and loved
> in a way surpassing anything men can imagine,
> loved before anyone had thought of you
> or spoken your name.

Rule for a New Brother (Springfield: Templegate, 1975), pp. 1-2.

11. ". . . anyone who seriously commits himself to prayer experiences its repercussion in every area of his life, so that it becomes less possible to think about prayer divorced from his life as a whole. . . . this pervasive experience is an experience of death and resurrection which draws us deeply into the Easter mystery of Christ." Maria Boulding, *Prayer: Our Journey Home* (Ann Arbor: Servant Books, 1979), p. 1.

12. There is no better caution here than that contained in the parable of the talents (Matt. 25:14-31). To him who has, Jesus explains, much more will be given — that is, if we willingly accept what we are given and build on it, we will grow into prayerful abundance. If we do not, the parable says, we will lose whatever we may have, little or much.

13. See Ann and Barry Ulanov, "Soul and Psyche," in *Religion and the Unconscious*, pp. 81-96.

14. An example of this approach is to be found in Ann Belford Ulanov, "What Do We Think People Are Doing When They Pray?," *Anglican Theological Review*, Vol. LX, No. 4, pp. 387-398.

CHAPTER TWO

1. Augustine says: "Following after God is the desire of happiness; to reach God is happiness itself." "A man is what his loves makes him." Prayer is "the affectionate reaching out of the mind for God." All cited in Hand, *Saint Augustine on Prayer*, p. 7.

2. ". . . desire directed toward God is the only power capable of raising the soul. Or rather, it is God alone who comes down and possesses the soul, but desire alone draws God down. He only comes to those who ask him to come; and he cannot refuse to come to those who implore him long, often, and ardently." Simone Weil, *Waiting for God*, trans. Emma Craufurd (New York: Capricorn, 1951), pp. 110-111.

    " . . . there is required for a subjective thinker imagination and feeling, dialectics in existential inwardness, together with passion. But passion first and last; for it is impossible to think about existence in existence without passion." Søren Kierkeggard, *Concluding Unscientific Postscript*, trans. David F. Swenson (Princeton: Princeton University Press, 1941), pp. 312-313.

3. We know from Freud that one aspect of our unconscious mental life is its infantile character and that it persists from our birth to our death. How can we exclude this aspect of the unconscious from our prayers? Will we remake creation in our preferred image?

4. "God wants you to tell Him all that afflicts you; do not remain silent then, devout Soul. As soon as some misfortune or some unpleasant accident befalls you come at once to make with due respect and humility your complaint to Him. If your trust is great, it will be enough that you place your misery before His eyes without asking Him to help you, enough if He is informed of what you suffer." Fr. Boutauld, *The Art of Conversing with God*, trans. J.D. Souza, S.J. (Rome: privately printed, 1959), pp. 5-6.

5. Hand, *St. Augustine on Prayer*, p. 10.

6. Prayer makes us aware of our capacity to pray and to meditate: "It follows that if God wants us to pray to him, this is in order that we may become aware of him and of ourselves, i.e., that we may achieve our own real being, and this implies an openness to all reality . . . . Such an awareness is not a luxury, it is essential to personal development. Apart from it man remains a mere *thing*, and might be caught up into the moving belt of unconscious causes." Maurice Nédoncelle, *The Nature and Use of Prayer*, trans. A. Manson (London: Burns Oates, 1962), p. 115.

7. Of course, it is good to emulate the lightness, the delicacy, the resilient sponginess of a soufflé in prayer, but never as a mere frivolity. There is always in prayer, however, the element of mortification, whether or not one follows the traditional injunctions to "cross" the "inclinations" of the senses, as Dom Augustine Baker puts it in the succinct seventeenth-century style of *Sancta Sophia, or Holy Wisdom* (New York: Dunigan, 1857), p. 147. The promptings of the spirit are often harsh and even when most enticing in their beckonings involve some roughness along the way. The roughness becomes bearable if we accept, as Francis de Sales suggests we do, Jesus's admonition to "eat what is set before you" (Luke 10:8). It is more virtuous, says Francis, to eat what is set before us — to take such spiritual promptings as may come to us — and to do so as it comes, whether we like it or not, than to look for the most disagreeable things as a scourging of ourselves. "Moreover, it is no small mortification to accommodate our taste to all kinds

of meat [or soufflé, we might add] and keep it in subjection to all kinds of occurrences." *Introduction to the Devout Life*, p. 133.

8. The scornful name of the Russian philosopher Lev Shestov for the formulas and constructions of the philosophers and the scientists and all other sources of "great truths" is Necessity (always with a capital *N*). He sees those who follow Necessity, even when presented in the august terms of an Aristotle or a Kant, as "eternal prisoners" of it. "To tear oneself away from its power, it is necessary 'to dare everything,' to accept the great and final struggle, to go forward without asking and without foreseeing what awaits us." That is what following the contrary movements of prayer brings. If we move toward the mystery of being, away from Necessity, we move toward a "primordial freedom," a "boundless free will which no 'knowledge' can contain . . . . Let the promise be realized," Shestov exhorts us. "'Nothing will be impossible for you!'" Lev Shestov, *Athens and Jerusalem*, trans. Bernard Martin (Athens: Ohio University Press, 1966), pp. 153, 154.

9. The reference here is to those writings of the so-called liberation theologians which challenge in their violent rhetoric the violence of the terrorists. For an opposing view, but not one that distorts liberation theology, see Edward Norman, *Christianity and the World Order* (Oxford: Oxford University Press, 1979), *passim*.

10. The great things God offers, according to St. Augustine, are the things that "make us blessed." Those are things that are meant to be "enjoyed" and not merely "used." The distinction is central not only for Augustine but for more than a thousand years of spirituality based on him, and it still has enduring psychological value. "Those things which are to be used," Augustine says, "help and, as it were, sustain us as we move toward blessedness in order that we may gain and cling to those things that make us blessed." If we make ends of those things that are merely to be used as means en route to our blessed enjoyment, "our course will be impeded and sometimes deflected, so that we are retarded in obtaining those things which are to be enjoyed, or even prevented altogether, shackled by an inferior love." See Saint Augustine, *On Christian Doctrine*, trans. D.W. Robertson, Jr. (Indianapolis: Bobbs-Merrill, 1958), p. 9.

11. "As the divine Spirit inspires us when he wills and as he wills, without subjecting himself to our evaluations and standards, similarly the true process of the mystical life cannot be confined to fixed rules, and one has to go almost entirely by the fruits, judging by them if things are from God or not." J. G. Arintero, O.P., *Stages in Prayer*, trans. Kathleen Pond (London:

Blackfriars, 1957), p. 8. See also *St. Ignatius's Own Story, As Told to Luis González de Cámara*, trans. William J. Young (Chicago: Loyola University Press, 1956), p. 10.

12. "The beginner must think of himself as one setting out to make a garden in which the Lord is to take his delight, yet in soil most unfruitful and full of weeds. His Majesty [God] uproots the weeds and will set good plants in their stead. Let us suppose that this is already done — that a soul has resolved to practise prayer and has already begun to do so. We have now, by God's help, like good gardeners, to make these plants grow, and to water them carefully, so that they may not perish, but may produce flowers which shall send forth great fragrance to give refreshment to this Lord of ours, so that He may often come into the garden to take His pleasure and have His delight among these virtues." *The Life of St. Teresa*, in *The Complete Works of St. Teresa of Jesus*, trans. and ed. E. Allison Peers (London: Sheed and Ward, 1957 [1944]), I, p. 65. This is from the first of a sequence of chapters in which Teresa's similitude of the water garden unfolds to contain a whole method of prayer, which mounts by degrees to union and rapture of the sort portrayed in Bernini's famous statue of the saint.

13. The consecrated procedure for the Fathers here was to follow desire into belief. We must follow "the Artisan who formed and fashioned us," Augustine says: "Every man wishes to understand. . . . Not all men, however, wish to believe. Imagine that a man says to me: 'Let me understand that I may believe.' I would answer: 'Believe that you may understand.'" *Selected Sermons of St. Augustine*, trans. Quincy Howe, Jr. (New York: Holt, Rinehart and Winston, 1966), p. 190.

14. It is a point Jesus makes often, as for example in John: "I can do nothing on my own authority; as I hear, I judge; and my judgment is just, because I seek not my own will but the will of him who sent me" (5:30). "For I have come down from heaven, not to do my own will, but the will of him who sent me . . ." (6:38).

15. "Prayer is the primary work of the moral and religious life. The root of this life is a free and conscious relationship with God, which then directs everything. It is the practise of prayer that expresses this free and conscious attitude towards God, just as the social contacts of daily life express our moral attitude towards our neighbour, and our ascetic struggles and spiritual efforts express our moral attitude towards ourselves. Our prayer reflects our attitude to God, and our attitude to God is reflected in prayer." From "What Is Prayer?" by Theophan the Recluse, the nineteenth-century Russian Orthodox Bishop who is a major source in *The Art of Prayer*, the Orthodox

Anthology compiled by Igumen [Abbot] Chariton of Valamo, trans. E. Kadloubovsky and E.M. Palmer (London: Faber, 1966), p. 61.

16. "It is a central secret of the spiritual life; it is a central secret of psychological health: One must love one's own way, no matter how awkward, and in one's own words, no matter how inadequate." Barry Ulanov, *The Making of a Modern Saint: A Biographical Study of Thérès' cf Lisieux* (New York: Doubleday, 1966), pp. 225-226.

17. "If you ask me how you are to begin, I must pray Almighty God, of his grace and courtesy, to tell you himself. Indeed, it is good for you to realize that I cannot teach you. It is not to be wondered at. For this is the work of God alone, deliberately wrought in whatever soul he chooses, irrespective of the merits of that particular soul." *The Cloud of Unknowing*, trans. Clifton Wolters (Baltimore: Penguin, 1970), p. 92.

18. Father Boutauld, *The Art of Conversing with God*, p. 5.

19. The depth psychologist Otto Rank, whose psychological system centered on the human will, describes it thus: "What is naturally and spontaneously effective in the transference situation and, rightly understood and handled, is also effective therapeutically, is the same thing that is potent in every relationship between two human beings, namely the will. Two wills clash, either the one overthrows the other or both struggle with and against one another for supremacy." Rank insists "that the neurotic above all learn to will, discover that he can will without getting guilt feeling on account of willing." Otto Rank, *Will Therapy and Truth and Reality* (New York: Knopf, 1968), pp. 7, 9.

20. Arintero says that God's Spirit enters us and works in us secretly, as if these gifts, in reality given by God, were our own: ". . . although it is in reality God who is working, he does so secretly under the veil of charity that it appears as if we had done all ourselves on our own account. . . ." *Stages in Prayer*, p. 7.

21. "Again I say, let us go into these waters ourselves; time flies by and waits not, and every man is responsible for himself. . . . we must go on working, because not to advance in the spiritual life is to go back." Brother Lawrence, *The Practice of the Presence of God*, trans. Donald Attwater (London: Burns Oates, 1948), p. 21. "It must not be understood . . . that all these things take place because once or twice God has granted a soul this favour; it must continue receiving them, for it is from their continuance that all our good proceeds. There is one earnest warning which I must give those who find themselves in this state: namely, that they exert the very greatest care

to keep themselves from occasions of offending God. For as yet the soul is not even weaned but is like a child beginning to suck the breast. If it be taken from its mother, what can it be expected to do but die? That, I am very much afraid, will be the lot of anyone to whom God has granted this favour if he gives up prayer; unless he does so for some very exceptional reason, or unless he returns to it quickly, he will go from bad to worse." St. Teresa of Avila, *The Interior Castle*, in *The Complete Works*, II, pp. 244-245.

22. False unconsciousness is the result of repressing materials from consciousness because we no not want to take responsibility for them. Jung emphasizes the importance of our willingness to respond openly and honestly to unconscious images and affects that appear in our awareness. Not only is this willingness important for our own psychic balance between consciousness and the unconscious, but it is a way we contribute to the task of civilizing psychic forces that occur in all of us. When we fail to take on the task, we set up false divisions in our own psychologies, between instinct and spirit, for example. But we also set up potentially dangerous tensions in society that often erupt in acts of violence, bizarre shootings by snipers or terrorists, or mass murders.

23. "Every kind of prayer which exists is set into motion by the impulses of the soul. . . . Every prayer is demand and request, or praise or thanksgiving. . . . Prayer is a beseeching for, a caring for, a longing for something, either liberation from evil things here or in the world to come, or a desire for promised things, or a demand for something by which man wishes to be brought nearer unto God. . . ." See Isaac of Nineveh, in *The Soul Afire*: *Revelations of the Mystics*, ed. H.A. Reinhold (New York: Pantheon, 1951), pp. 302-303.

24. "God is prepared to be outside [our life], He is prepared to take it up completely as a cross, but He is not prepared to be simply a part of our life." Anthony Bloom, *Beginning to Pray* (New York: Paulist Press, 1970), p. 6.

CHAPTER THREE

1. The processes of projection and its natural accompaniment, introjection, are accepted by depth psychologists of all schools as fundamental to our psychic life. From the first weeks of life, we send out into the world fantasy images of our experience of our own instincts in relation to the world, projections. We take in from the world and people around us images and experiences of them and of parts of them, introjections. This ceaseless interaction is a basic

process in the creation of a self in relation to a world. Both self and world are made up of real experience of real objects (people) and fantasies about those objects, about our own body, and our own mental processes. Psychologists talk about these basic ingredients in different vocabularies. Melanie Klein talks about internalized objects and external objects. Jung talks about archetypal images and personal images. Freud talks about introjections and projections.

"The self-aware, organized contemplation of external objects — a contemplation that both preserves the external index of these objects and recognizes itself for what it is, that is, thought — is one of the most impressive aspects of psychic development. The capacity for such contemplation is not given; it calls urgently for explanation. . . . It is the task of accounting for the usual increasing sway of the secondary process over the primary process during psychological development, or of the reality principle over the pleasure principle, or of the mature ego over the id and infantile ego and superego." Roy Schafer, *Aspects of Internalization* (New York: International Universities Press, 1968), p. 137.

For the religious person, this capacity to contemplate might be summed up as the ability to see the other as *other*, an ability that depends psychologically and spiritually on the possession of a self in both its conscious and unconscious aspects. In its most developed expression, seeing the other directs one's gaze to the unfathomable otherness of God.

2. See Sigmund Freud, *The Future of an Illusion*, trans. W.D. Robson-Scott (New York: Liveright, 1953), pp. 24, 29, 34, 38.

3. For an excellent summery of these views, see Bowker, *The Sense of God*, pp. 22-43.

4. Clearly we must not allow ourselves in the purgation of prayer to be tempted, as Paul Evdokimov points out the early martyrs and ascetics of the desert were, to imitate Christ crucified or to take "literally the counsels of the Gospel: 'If thy hand . . . thy foot . . . are an occasion of sin for thee, cut them off. . . .' " But it is equally clear, as Evdokimov says, that "the soul that has been drawn from nothingness desires to find its origins and asks to be recreated, to allow itself to be unmade and remade by having its elements purified one after another." Paul Evdokimov, *The Struggle with God*, trans. Sister Gertrude, O.P. (Glen Rock: Paulist Press, 1966), pp. 100, 101. The great danger, as Evdokimov says earlier in his instructive book, is the susceptibility "of the man who is totally ignorant of his interior life. In moments of solitude or of suffering, he has no social formula to protect him or to solve the conflicts in his soul" (p. 45). The great hope of this stripping

that begins in prayer is that we will find ourselves and our source and will never again be so vulnerable.

5. Melanie Klein writes that "the ego functions from the beginning and . . . among its first activities are the defense against anxiety and the use of processes of introjection and projection." "The Mutual Influences in the Development of Ego and Id," in *Envy and Gratitude*, p. 57.

6. "Unless completely repressed and isolated defensively from its complex roots, the representation of God, like any other, is reshaped, refined, and retouched throughout life. With aging the question of the existence of God becomes a personal matter to be faced or avoided. For most people the occasion for deciding on the final representation of their God comes in contemplating their own impending death." Anna-Maria Rizzuto, *The Birth of the Living God*, p. 8.

7. Even if we have been drawn to contemplate the Creator, as Hugh of Saint-Victor insists, we must begin with "the consideration of created things. . . ." God is at first adorned in the clothing we give him, in our images, in our needs, in our projections. It is, says Hugh, "a sort of wrestling-match [that] goes on between ignorance and knowledge, and the light of truth somehow flickers in the midst of all the darkness of error." Finally the flame of truth burns clearly, "all the smoke clears, the darkness is dispelled. . . ." "The Soul's Three Ways of Seeing," in Hugh of Saint-Victor, *Selected Spiritual Writings*, trans. by a Religious of C.S.M.V. (London: Faber, 1962), p. 184. Until the moment that the clear flame blazes forth, we should not be dismayed by the fact that the smoke and the flame must go together, by the fact that we have needs.

8. People describe this encounter with otherness in individual ways. Jung, for example, writes of it as the objectivity of the psyche: "Now that vision of God . . . is the experience of the living presence and the absolute objectivity of the psyche. . . . If you can train yourself to the point of being able to experience psychical contents as objective, then you can feel a psychical presence, for then you know that the psychical contents are not things you have made. They occur, and so you are not alone in the psychical world. . . . This experience of the objective fact is all important, because it denotes the presence of something which is not I, yet is still psychical. Such an experience can reach a climax where it becomes an experience of God. Even the smallest thing of that kind has a mana quality, a divine quality. It is fascinating. A bit more and it is the whole deity, the giver of life. It is a decisive experience. . . . " C. G. Jung, *The Visions Seminars* (Zürich: Spring Publications, 1976), I, pp. 72-73. Jacob Boehme, the sixteenth-century

mystic, describes his image of otherness in terms of an eye looking back at him. This image first came to Boehme when he looked at his reflection in a pewter dish and saw his own eye mirrored there beholding him. This eye became a vision of an inner other — the soul looking at him much as God would, and yet also reflecting his own face. Thus the soul bridges God and the self. This same image can be found in his description of Sophia as the mirror of divinity. See Jacob Boehme, *The Way to Christ*, trans. Peter Erb (New York: Paulist Press, 1978), p. 6.

9. "When we say our God is love, we can be sure it is a compensation; we know it is not true. We say it to compensate the fact that we do not love enough, that we hate too much. Our ideal is love because we are too separated. People talk of community and relationship because they have none; they always talk of the things they do not possess. . . . The way people define their God is most characteristic." C.G. Jung, *The Visions Seminars*, I, p. 72.

10. These important totem objects exist in a special space between the infant and mother, and between the adult self and others. The psychoanalyst D.W. Winnicott is noted for his exploration of this "transitional space." He writes: "This intermediate area of experience, unchallenged in respect of its belonging to inner or external (shared) reality, constitutes the greater part of the infant's experience, and throughout life is retained in the intense experiencing that belongs to the arts and to religion and to imaginative living, and to creative scientific work." D.W. Winnicott, *Playing and Reality* (London: Tavistock, 1971), p. 14.

11. The poetry of the great apostles of prayer is very much their own, inflected according to the customs of their time, the habits of their culture, their own temperaments. And so we must understand, as Eric Colledge reminds us in his introduction to his translation of Ruysbroeck, that Ruysbroeck and John of the Cross did not mean to convey with the image of darkness "any conception of doubt, despair, or tribulation. . . ." Rather it is a way of indicating, and an incomparable one, that the largest knowledge of God does not come through the senses or thought. "One must not seek to understand God's mysteries: they are to be accepted through faith, not comprehension. . . ." Ruysbroeck, *The Spiritual Espousals* (New York: Harper, n.d.), pp. 33, 35.

12. Modern speculation on the nature of images and symbols reaches across all the humanistic disciplines and presents us with every kind of assertion about our own nature as symbol-making and image-receiving creatures. The speculations, in spite of the modernity of the language and the comparative youth of some of the disciplines, are not new ones. As long ago as the fourth century St. Augustine was working out a semiotics that insisted on taking every sign

and symbol back to an originating *thing*, every puff of smoke to its source of fire, in his *De doctrina Christiana*, and behind him stood the large related speculations of St. Paul, Cicero, Plato, and Aristotle. The reasoning is inevitably teleological, from effect back to cause. If we do not take the effect as an end in itself, an uncaused effect, we stand a prayerful chance of getting to the true Uncaused Cause.

13. "Consider," says Richard of Saint-Victor, "how easy it is for the human soul at any time to reproduce the shape of any kind of thing in the imagination and to make any kind of original creature, as often as he wills, independent of pre-existing matter and as it were, from nothing." From this consideration, Richard suggests, we may be able to understand how God, reserving "to himself the truth of things . . . has conceded to his image the power of forming images of things at any time. . . ." In *Selected Writings on Contemplation*, trans. Clare Kirchberger (New York: Harper, n.d.), pp. 172-173. We get to "the truth of things" through certain particular images, such as Jacob's ladder, with the aid of those special readers of the images who pray their way from sign and symbol to things. Francis de Sales, for example, sees the rungs of Jacob's ladder as "the various degrees of charity by which we advance from virtue to virtue" and those on the ladder as "either men who have angelical hearts or angels who have human bodies. . . . They have wings to soar up to God by holy prayer, but they have also feet to walk with men in a holy and edifying way of life." *Introduction to the Devout Life*, p. 5. For Pico della Mirandola, some centuries before Francis, the ladder is the supreme figure for understanding the ascents and descents of philosophy in its contemplative pursuit of the sacred mysteries: "Using philosophy through the steps of the ladder, that is of nature, and penetrating all things from center to center, we shall sometimes descend, with titanic force rending the unity like Osiris into many parts, and we shall sometimes ascend, with the force of Phoebus collecting the parts like the limbs of Osiris into a unity, until resting at last in the bosom of the Father who is above the ladder, we shall be made perfect with the felicity of theology." Giovanni Pico della Mirandola, "Oration on the Dignity of Man," trans. E. L. Forbes, in Ernst Cassirer et al., *The Renaissance Philosophy of Man* (Chicago: Phoenix Books, 1948 [1945]), p. 230.

14. Søren Kierkegaard, *Philosophical Fragments*, trans. David F. Swenson (Princeton: Princeton University Press, 1936), pp. 19-21 in particular.

15. See Ruysbroeck, *The Spiritual Espousals*, pp. 179-181.

16. There is a large and distinguished scholarship devoted to the parables of Jesus, but can it ever go much beyond the wisdom of Boccaccio in the

fourteenth century, defending what he calls the "veil of fiction" against the accusation, among other things, of superficiality? For him, fiction "under guise of invention, illustrates or proves an idea. . . ." He associates the parables of "Christ, who is God," with the work of Virgil and Homer, who "seem to be writing history," but whose "hidden meaning is far other than appears on the surface." He also invokes the comic poets Terence and Plautus who, though directing their lines to nothing but literal meanings, "portray varieties of human nature and conversation, incidentally teaching the reader and putting him on his guard. If the events they describe have not actually taken place, yet since they are common, they could have occurred, or might at some time." *Boccaccio on Poetry*, trans. Charles G. Osgood (Indianapolis: Bobbs-Merrill, 1956 [1930]), pp. 48-49.

CHAPTER FOUR

1. Even so comparatively gentle a spiritual counselor as the eighteenth-century Jesuit Father Grou cannot help a minatory tone in these precincts. The theme is renunciation of everything that is not immediately identifiable as from God and of God: "I am made for God alone." We must seek and find "purity of intention" and "renounce without exception everything that is not God alone." At the same time, happily, Father Grou remembers the words of Scripture: "He will not suffer you to be tempted above that you are able to bear." J. N. Grou, *Manual for Interior Souls* (London: Burns Oates, 1952 [1892]), pp. 159, 227ff., 260, 171-172.

2. Nédoncelle says prayer begins with inward recollection which is withdrawal from fantasy as well as the world: "Withdrawal from the world, withdrawal from one's personal fantasies, this means that by a two-fold renunciation we free ourselves from the spell of the world of nature and make ourselves ready and disposed for an act of inner attention . . . . For to what are we supposed to pay attention? To ourself? We have just seen that the ego is equivocal, and provides a problem rather than a solution. Prayer cannot be content with this. It requires silence, but it is not narcissistic recollection." Nédoncelle, *The Nature and Use of Prayer*, p. 89. For many contemporary people, this exclusion of fantasy elements in the initial recollecting work of prayer breeds guilt and discouragement that often lead to a cessation of any effort to pray. We suggest another route, one that includes fantasy but does not stop there. The relief that many persons taking this approach experience may indicate the wisdom of this path.

3. Thomas Merton, *The Climate of Monastic Prayer* (Spencer: Cistercian Publications, 1969), p. 20.

4. Having a confessor or spiritual director is especially helpful in dealing with our blind spots since it is much easier for another person to see them. However, St. Teresa's caution must also be remembered — virtue and learning are equally important in one who offers spiritual counsel. Neither is much good without the other. See *The Life of St. Teresa* in *The Collected Works*, I, pp. 80-82.

5. Melanie Klein asserts on the basis of her observations of very young children that envy and greed exist in us from birth. She defines them thus: "Envy is the angry feeling that another person possesses and enjoys something desirable — the envious impulse being to take it away or to spoil it. . . . Greed is an impetuous and insatiable craving, exceeding what the subject needs and what the object is able and willing to give." *Envy and Gratitude and Other Works, 1946-1963*, p. 181. We all must come to terms with these emotions. We can either deny them or acknowledge and integrate them with our loving feelings.

6. Merton, *op. cit.*, p. 144.

7. Perhaps the boldest claim for the imagination, and thus for images, is Coleridge's in the *Biographia Literaria*, where it is seen as either primary or secondary: "The primary imagination I hold to be the living power and prime agent of all human perception, and as a repetition in the finite mind of the eternal act of creation in the infinite I AM. The secondary I consider as an echo of the former, co-existing with the conscious will, yet still as identical with the primary in the kind of its agency, and differing only in degree, and in the mode of its operation. It dissolves, diffuses, dissipates, in order to re-create; or where this process is rendered impossible, yet still, at all events, it struggles to idealize and to unify. It is essentially *vital*, even as all objects (as objects) are essentially fixed and dead." Samuel Taylor Coleridge, *Biographia Literaria*, ed. George Watson (London: Everyman, 1965), p. 167. Coleridge sees the imagination as a "reconciling and mediating power," as he puts it elsewhere (in an appendix to *The Statesman's Manual*), which "incorporating the reason in the images of sense . . . gives birth to a system of symbols, harmonious in themselves and cosubstantial with the truths of which they are conductors." The images of art may bring us to the very center of being. Prayer without their reconciling and mediating force loses much of its grace and some of its meaning. (Thus the appendix to this book, with its listing of examples of what the arts may offer as aids, supports, and openings to prayer.)

8. A particularly rich gathering of such poetry is to be found in any representative anthology of the English metaphysical poets of the seventeenth century. See for example *George Herbert and the Seventeenth-Century Religious Poets*, ed. Mario A. Di Cesare (New York: Norton, 1978), with its substantial selections from Herbert, Crashaw, Marvell, Vaughan, and Traherne. The bits and pieces of poetry one finds in anthologies that cover anything much larger in period or numbers of poets are not equally persuasive as examples of the reconciling and mediating imagination, however effective this or that poem may be. Best of all are the well-edited, fully annotated editions of poets like Hopkins, Herbert, and Traherne, where a passing comment in enlargement of a difficult or mottled text may lead directly to meditation.

9. Traherne says it well in "Insatiableness":

> 'Tis mean Ambition to desire
>   A single World:
>   To many I aspire,
>   Though one upon another hurl'd:
> Nor will they all, if they be all confin'd,
>   Delight my Mind.

The esthetics of prayer are not those of naturalism. Its reality, to use a felicitous phrase of the poet Wallace Stevens, is "of the most august imagination."

10. In a conversation with Barry Ulanov, Rothko marveled over what he had learned in the endless texturings of interiority which make up the great darkness of his paintings, and again over the color, somewhere in the red-purple-brown area of the spectrum, which he settled upon as a painted frame for the black. He marveled, but he did not attempt to find words to explain or develop any further what the paintings "say" so well.

11. See Chang Chung-yuan, *Creativity and Taoism* (New York: Harper Colophon Books, 1970 [1963]), pp. 104-105. Professor Chang neither overestimates the insights of the East nor underestimates those of the West. He makes good use of Jung's understanding of the "non-ego-like-self" (see pp. 121-122) and draws rich insights from Taoism which support his quotation from Whitehead near the end of his book: "Art at its highest exemplifies the metaphysical doctrine of the interweaving of absoluteness upon relativity" (p. 237; quoted from *Adventures in Ideas*). This is a doctrine which we hope we have made commendable in *this* book.

12. "A period may intervene when the word to which we are holding (or it may be our *consciousness* of a naked intent towards God) has disappeared, and

we are left either in blankness, or in what we have described earlier as involuntary distraction. The point to note is that it is only as we are emerging from this period that we recognize it for what it is. If we now find that our mind has been engaged on something other than God we are not to be concerned about that, or to think that our prayer has gone wrong. On the contrary we should accept this as the Holy Spirit's work." Robert Llewelyn, *The Positive Role of Distraction in Prayer* (Oxford: Sisters of the Love of God Press, 1977), p. 3. Llewelyn does caution his readers not to turn this involuntary distraction into a voluntary one by pursuing it too far.

13. The movement from identification with our images to disidentification is perfectly caught by T.S. Eliot in *East Coker*, the second of his *Four Quartets*. First there is

> The wild thyme unseen and the wild strawberry,
> The laughter in the garden, echoed ecstasy

— and then, in paraphrase of John of the Cross:

> In order to arrive there,
> To arrive where you are, to get from where you are not,
> You must go by a way wherein there is no ecstasy.
> In order to arrive at what you do not know
> You must go by a way which is the way of ignorance.
> In order to possess what you do not possess
> You must go by the way of dispossession.

All of which brings Eliot to Good Friday and the figure of "the wounded surgeon," Christ on the Cross.

14. What is involved is a long inner conversation, in which what was good and freeing in our fantasies is acknowledged and what had become too possessive in them is also acknowledged. We move to hold but not to be held, and all with that sense of "the divine presence in the stillness of [our] own heart, in the deepest recesses of [our] soul" which, for Heiler, defines "religious genius." For, as he says, "it is always the reverential and trustful consciousness of the living presence of God, which is the keynote of the genuine prayer-experience," and this is an experience that can come only in and through prayer. See Friedrich Heiler, *Prayer*, trans. and ed. Samuel McComb and J.E. Park (New York: Oxford University Press, 1932), p. 356.

15. "It is impossible to remain for ever in a state of spiritual exaltation God allows certain intermissions in our fervour because he does not wish either to deprive us of the courage by which we climb higher, or to feed the pride which leads us to fall   The essence of prayer does not just consist in those feelings of joy which sometimes accompany it. Loving prayer may some-

times exist without such feelings; and this is a more purified and disinterested form of prayer, since, being deprived of spiritual joy, its goal is God alone." Alexander Elchaninov, *The Diary of a Russian Priest*, trans. Helen Iswolsky (London: Faber, 1967), p. 171.

CHAPTER FIVE

1. One sees this movement from self-conscious exercise to free movement, free even when carefully choreographed, in the work of any first-rate dancer and in almost any kind of dance, from ballet and modern dance to jazz dancing. The same remarkable development — so much like the progress we make in the world of primary speech and often motivated by it — is to be found in the growth of a choreographer. José Limon, himself a fine example of that sort of development, says it well in describing the work of that master of the American dance, Doris Humphrey, who "saw that the dance idiom she sought would have to be invented. Its creation would be a hard and long voyage of discovery into the inner self; its origins, its awareness and experience and capacity as an American self living in the twentieth century." José Limon, "An American Accent," in *The Modern Dance*, ed. S. J. Cohen (Middletown: Wesleyan University Press, 1969), pp. 21-23.

2. This relation to fantasy is very different from repressing it. In repression, we lose touch altogether with the fantasy; it is as if it had never existed; we do not know about it at all; it is unconscious. Here, we do know about the fantasy; it is related to consciousness; we are aware of it if we need to be or choose to be. But we are not caught by it, feeling compelled to go over and over it in our minds. We accept it as part of ourselves and can put it aside, giving our attention to something else. In this way we are disidentified from the fantasy. For discussion of such "disidentification," see Ann and Barry Ulanov, *Religion and the Unconscious*, pp. 188-190.

3. Plotinus, that master of a metaphysics built on the interior life, says: "We always move round the One, but we do not always fix our gaze upon it: we are like a choir of singers who stand round the conductor, but do not always sing in time because their attention is diverted to some external object; when they look at the conductor they sing well and are really with him. So we always move round the One; if we did not, we should be dissolved and no longer exist; but we do not always look towards the One. When we do, we attain the end of our existence, and our repose, and we no longer sing out of tune, but form in very truth a divine chorus round the One." See W. R.

Inge, *The Philosophy of Plotinus* (London: Longmans, Green, 1948), pp. 138-139.

4. See Jürgen Moltmann, *Theology of Play* (New York: Harper & Row, 1972), p. 21.

5. The Vedantist Swami Prabhavananda, though arguing for a particular religious practice, make the point very well for all religion: "There exist a number of facets, as it were, to the infinite God. He can be loved and worshipped and meditated upon through any of these facets. . . . He is with form and without form; He is personal and impersonal, and beyond; He is absolute existence, absolute knowledge, and absolute bliss; and He is the indefinable, inexpressible Reality. . . . There is a Hindu prayer which says: 'They call you by so many names; they divide you, as it were, by different names, yet in each one of these is to be found your omnipotence. You are reached through any of these.'" Swami Prabhavananda, *Religion in Practice* (Hollywood: Vedanta Press, 1968), p. 164.

6. See Jacob Boehme, *The Way to Christ*, pp. 29, 68, 83; see Brother Lawrence, *The Practice of the Presence of God*, pp. 31-32.

7. See J. J. Stoudt, *Jacob Boehme: His Life and Thought* (New York: Seabury, 1968 [1957]), p. 119.

8. The God-centered American writer Flannery O'Connor was also a God-questioning woman and writer. She saw the physical direction and geographical locus forced upon her by a fatal illness as impossibly confining. She questioned the forced return to the South with all her being. Questioning God, she reached God: "O'Connor greets as a spiritual death sentence the news that she would have to spend the rest of her life at home in the South. . . . But there is no doubt she made a complete turn-about, coming to regard the South not as the place where she had been, but where she was *supposed* to be." Ralph C. Wood, "Talent Increased and Returned to God: Flannery O'Connor's Letters," *Anglican Theological Review*, Vol. LXII, No. 2, April 1980, p. 163.

9. The important thing, as Bernard Lonergan says, is not the answer, but the question: "However much religious or irreligious answers differ, however much there differ the questions they explicitly raise, still at their root there is the same transcendental tendency of the human spirit that questions, that questions without restriction, that questions the significance of its own questioning, and so comes to the question of God. . . . There lies within [human] horizon a region for the divine, a shrine for ultimate holiness. It cannot be ignored. The atheist may pronounce it empty. The agnostic may

urge that he finds his investigation has been inconclusive. The contemporary humanist will refuse to allow the question to arise. But their negations presuppose the spark in our clod, our native orientation to the divine." Bernard J. F. Lonergan, S. J., *Method in Theology* (New York: Herder and Herder, 1972), p. 103.

10. The process of disidentifying is experienced as a series of lettings go of our tight hold upon anything we hold most dear, anything we feel is absolutely necessary to us. In letting go we do not lose that thing, but we radically change our relationship to it. It is no longer equated with us, the center of our identity. Instead, it is now only one part of what we are, no longer the definition of who we were. In psychological language this is the process of ego-differentiation; in religious language, it is the process of achieving detachment. An example is a mother's love for her child that moves from her identification with the child as part of herself to recognition of the child as other than herself. She loves the child throughout, but after disidentification does not have to possess the child.

11. Hans Urs von Balthasar, *Prayer*, trans. A. V. Littledale (New York: Sheed & Ward, 1961), p. 73. See also pp. 20, 30, 68-72.

12. The intensity of the approach to God's mystery should not be under-estimated. For as Jung says, "Religion is a relationship to the highest or strongest value, be it positive or negative." Accepting "consciously, the value by which [they] are possessed unconsciously," people who had such a religious experience "came to themselves, they could accept themselves and by this they were also reconciled to adverse circumstances and events. This is much like what was formerly expressed by saying: He has made his peace with God, he has sacrificed his will, he has submitted himself to the will of God." C. G. Jung, *Psychology and Religion* (New Haven: Yale University Press, 1938), pp. 98-99.

13. It may also be that what seemed threatening in those dry periods was not abandonment on God's part, but simply a significant pause in an intimate conversation, an enriching silence. Kierkegaard's understanding here is large: "Oh, in the time of silence when man remains alone, abandoned when he does not hear Thy voice, it seems to him doubtless that the separation must last forever. Oh, in the time of silence when man consumes himself in the desert in which he does not hear Thy voice, it seems to him doubtless that it is completely extinguished. Father in Heaven! It is only a moment of silence in an intimacy of conversation. Bless then this silence as Thy word to man; grant that he never forgets that Thou speakest also when Thou art silent; give him this consolation if he waits on Thee, that Thou art silent

through love, so that in Thy silence as in Thy word Thou art still the same Father and that it is still the same paternal love that Thou guidest by Thy voice and that Thou doest instruct by Thy silence." See *The Prayers of Kierkegaard*, ed. P. D. LeFevre (Chicago: University of Chicago Press, 1956), 64, "Thy Silence," p. 76.

14. See *The Spiritual Life: A Summary of the Instructions on the Virtues and on Prayer Given by Saint Jane Frances Fremyot de Chantal* (St. Louis: Herder, 1928), p. 104. "He told our Sisters of Lyons that in these words everything was comprised. The last three years of his life he repeated them unceasingly. . . ."

CHAPTER SIX

1. Wayne Oates says that silence does not come easily to most of us: "Silence is not native to my world. Silence, more than likely, is a stranger to your world, too. If you and I ever have silence in our noisy hearts, we are going to have to grow it. . . . we will do so on silence's terms for growth — terms which are not yet our own." Wayne Oates, *Nurturing Silence in a Noisy Heart* (Garden City: Doubleday, 1979), p. 3. The psychoanalyst Masud Khan describes a case in which the patient used silence to communicate his problems: "The primary function of his silence was to communicate through the transference and the analytic process a very disturbed early childhood relationship to his mother which had brought about identity diffusion. . . . The persistent silence was also a mode of acting out and served the functions of recollecting, integrating and working through the pathogenic early relationship to the mother. . . . " M. Masud Khan, *The Privacy of the Self* (New York: International Universities Press, 1974), pp. 168-169.

2. We turn night into day with such fear-centered restlessness, holding on to the noise of our waking hours and repelling night and sleep, God's "most beautiful creations," according to the French poet Charles Péguy. There is no denying at such moments that we humans are, as Péguy calls us, monsters of anxiety, wells of disquiet — more restless in ourselves, he says, "than all creation put together." See "Sleep," in Charles Péguy, *Basic Verities*, trans. Anne and Julian Green (New York: Pantheon, 1943), pp. 208-215, and "Night," in Charles Péguy, *Men and Saints*, trans. Anne and Julian Green (New York: Pantheon, 1944), pp. 272-299. As with everything in these volumes, both poems are presented in French and English.

3. See *The Diaries of Franz Kafka 1910-1913,* ed. Max Brod (New York: Schocken Books, 1948), pp. 264-265.

4. The reference here is to that great prophetic novel of Dostoevsky that is still, perhaps, better known as *The Possessed* than as *The Devils,* which is the correct translation of the Russian title. We miss some of the meaning and much of the prayerful strength of the book if we move with the more familiar title away from the demons to concentrate on the demoniacs. The source is, after all, the episode of the Gadarene swine (Matt. 8:28-33), which is surely meant to remind us, as Kafka says, that there is no well-being for us as long as we are filled with our "many devils."

5. See "The Leaden Echo and the Golden Echo," in *The Poems of Gerard Manley Hopkins,* ed. W. H. Gardner and N.H. MacKenzie (New York: Oxford University Press, 1967), pp. 91-93.

6. See Franz Kafka, *Letters to Felice,* ed. Erich Heller and Jürgen Born, trans. James Stern and Elizabeth Duckworth (New York: Schocken Books, 1973), pp. 185-186.

7. "The answer surely is that we who are still on this side of the veil, have direct and real knowledge of the manner in which God's grace and mercy operate, even though in this life only," says Baron von Hügel in the midst of a discussion of hell. "We are able roughly to follow some of the main outlines of these orderings by God Himself of God's own generosities and gifts." We can see, says von Hügel, how our impure and untrue and cruel words, thoughts, and acts, our "cowardly shrinking from . . . our own best insight and special grace, relax or strain, or harden or deflect, our own inclinations, habits, and acts. . . ." We can also find repentance, which "at any degree of depth, will be a grace of God through Christ. . . ." But what we need most is an act of "pure love," and here von Hügel invokes that great ally of our low moments, the Good Thief crucified next to Christ. See Baron Friederich von Hügel, *Essays and Addresses on the Philosphy of Religion* (London: Dent, 1963 [1921]), I, pp. 202-203.

8. Addressed to the individual in his solitude, Kierkegaard's book, *Purity of Heart Is To Will One Thing,* directs his "individual" to face God because "Only the Eternal is always appropriate and always present, is always true." See *Purity of Heart,* trans. Douglas V. Steere (New York: Harpers, 1938), p. 3.

9. See Max Picard, *The World of Silence,* trans. Stanley Godman (Chicago: Regnery, 1952), pp. 219, 227, 229-230.

10. The experience of a numinous silence, looking toward God, is masterfully communicated in the last pages of Hermann Broch's novel, *The Death of Virgil,* trans. Jean Starr Untermeyer (New York: Pantheon, 1945). These are some of his words which come so close to saying the unsayable: "The no thing filled the emptiness and it became the universe. . . . the word hovered over the universe, over the nothing, floating beyond the expressible, beyond the inexpressible. . . . the more he penetrated into the flooding sound and was penetrated by it, the more unattainable, the greater, the graver and more elusive became the word. . . . it was the word beyond speech" (pp. 481-482). "What we cannot speak about," says the philosopher Ludwig Wittgenstein in the famous ending to his *Tractatus Logico-Philosophicus,* "we must consign to silence." See the translation by D. F. Pears and B. F. McGuinness (London: Routledge, 1961), p. 151.

11. Another way of putting this is to remind ourselves that every Omega point (to use Teilhard de Chardin's vivid metaphor), every grand convergence, must be preceded by a horde of Alphas, Betas, and Gammas. If we begin to see in our dialogues with the past as well as the present, our meetings with tradition as well as the new, that where we are is in a vast purposeful continuum that remains somehow approachable, then our prayers, whether filled with words or silence, will be graced, for we will be in touch with those who have known grace.

12. In his little treatise on *The Christian Life,* Augustine is adamant about the kinds of experience, from the obvious sins to the obvious virtues, from an easy moral life to a suffering one, that can be seen reflected in a religious person's demeanor. Anything false will show. "A man of God should so appear and conduct himself that there would be no one who would not desire to see him, no one who would not wish to hear him, no one who, having seen him, would not believe he was a son of God. . . ." See *The Christian Life,* trans. Sister Mary Sarah Muldowney, S. S. J., in St. Augustine, *Treatises on Various Subjects,* ed. R. J. Deferrari (New York: Fathers of the Church, 1952), p. 26. For Boehme, true suffering, astringent as it is, always produces a sweet fruit. "The bitter quality. . . maketh the tree moveable or stirring," he says in the allegorical language of *The Aurora,* "so that it *springeth* and groweth green and flourisheth, and so getteth its branches, leaves and fruit." There is no doubt in Boehme's mind about human corruption; he sees the individual "*half* dead" and impossible of perfection, at least here below. But he also sees man becoming "enlightened and kindled by the Holy Ghost" and the "heat" of growth "generated through the power and impulse of the astringent and bitter qualities.   " See *The Aurora,*

trans. John Sparrow (London: Clarke, 1960), pp. 199-201. The true cross, as distinguished from the false, builds, and builds love, and a loving appearance that all can recognize, not unrest. It offers no promises but yields its fruit instead.

13. Interior poverty is one of the defining textures of faith. It is that ineffable but not inaccessible renunciation of both certainty and certitude, of all the smug satisfactions, not the least of them self-satisfaction, which is summed up in a brief rabbinical statement: "Elijah said, 'God looked about among all good qualities to give to Israel, and he found nothing better than poverty.' So people say, 'Poverty suits Israel as a red bridle suits a white horse' (*Hagigah* 9ᵇ)." See C. G. Montefoore and H. Loewe, *A Rabbinic Anthology* (New York: Meridian, 1960 [1938]), pp. 445-446.

14. Melanie Klein formulated the concept of "reparation" as a distinct achievement in a person's development. She describes it thus: "When the infant feels that his destructive impulses and phantasies are directed against the complete person of his loved object, guilt arises in full strength, and, together with it, the over-riding urge to repair, preserve or revive the loved injured object. . . . the tendency to make reparation ultimately derives from the life instinct. . . ." Melanie Klein, *Envy and Gratitude and Other Works, 1946-1963*, p. 74.

15. See Konstantin Leontiev, *Against the Current: Selected Writings*, ed. George Ivask, trans. George Reavey (New York: Weybright & Talley, 1969), pp. 22-23.

16. Dostoevsky has his formidable Grand Inquisitor say to Jesus, "know that I fear Thee not. . . . I too prized the freedom with which Thou hast blessed men, and I too was striving to stand among Thy elect. . . . But I awakened and would not serve madness. I turned back and joined the ranks of those *who have corrected Thy work.*" Fyodor Dostoevsky, *The Brothers Karamazov*, trans. Constance Garnett (New York: New American Library, 1957), p. 240.

CHAPTER SEVEN

1. An excellent general introduction to aggression is found in Anthony Storr, *Human Aggression* (New York: Atheneum, 1968). See also Erich Fromm, *The Anatomy of Human Destructiveness* (New York: Holt, Rinehart and Winston, 1973).

2. In "the Divine judgment," says Gregory the Great, "it is just that they, who neglect to consider and guard the power of piety, should be deceived by the odour of their own fancy." That is not so much a harsh judgment on the medieval theologian's part as a facing of facts. The sort of self-righteousness that constantly provides us with excuses for our limitations bedevils *us* most of all, whatever it may do to others with whom we come in contact. See St. Gregory the Great, *Morals on the Book of Job* (Oxford: Parker, 1850), III, 644.

3. For a thorough discussion of the passive deployment of aggression, see Edrita Fried, *Active/Passive: the Crucial Psychological Dimension* (New York: Grune and Stratton, 1970).

4. The God of our aggression is the Lord of Psalm 139, the one whom we address by saying:

> O LORD, thou hast searched me and known me!
>> Thou knowest when I sit down and when I rise up;
>>> thou discernest my thoughts from afar.

There is no fleeing this Lord, not on earth, not in heaven, not in hell. He formed us inwardly and outwardly; he knew us, he knows us, from unformed substance through the last moment in the book of our days. We can say to the God of our aggression,

> O that thou wouldst slay the wicked, O God,
>> And that men of blood would depart from me,
> men who maliciously defy thee,
>> Who lift themselves up against thee for evil!
> Do I not hate them that hate thee, O LORD?

In such a tumultuous setting, with such cries of vengeance, we can even dare to say,

> Search me, O God, and know my heart!
>> Try me and know my thoughts!
> And see if there be any wicked way in me,
>> And lead me in the way everlasting!

5. Melanie Klein made the daring assertion that at certain phases of development young children have sadistic fantasies about loved persons in the family. Under great stress, adults may again experience such sadism. By and large, however, these sadistic fantasies exist in us unconsciously and express themselves only indirectly. She writes: "The assumption that the extravagant phantasies which arise in a very early stage of the child's development never become conscious could well help to explain the phenomenon that the child

expresses its sadistic impulses toward real objects only in an attenuated form
. . . toward inanimate things, small animals and so on." Melanie Klein, *The Psychoanalysis of Children*, trans. Alix Strachey (New York: Delacorte/Seymour Lawrence, 1975), p. 151.

6. See Sigmund Freud, *Civilization and Its Discontents*, trans. Joan Riviere (London: Hogarty, 1955), pp. 23, 52; see also Freud, *The Future of an Illusion*, pp. 17, 31-33, 74.

7. The psychoanalyst Esther Menaker gives convincing evidence that such a devaluing of ourselves in fact functions as a defense against a greater suffering that lurks underneath — an experience of not being loved and found lovable. We would rather blame ourselves than face that loss: ". . . masochistic self-devaluation originates at the oral level of infantile development . . . the outcome of traumatic deprivation . . . a defence against experiencing this deprivation with its concomitant anxiety and aggression. . . ." Esther Menaker, *Masochism and the Emergent Ego* (New York: Human Sciences Press, 1979), p. 57.

8. Karen Horney's expressive phrase "the tyranny of the shoulds" sums up this sort of self-victimization. We reject the person we really are and try to impose on ourselves what we think we should be — a host of unattainable and contradictory ideals, such as boundless patience and vigorous self-assertion, endless love and complete independence from others. See Karen Horney, *Neurosis and Human Growth* (New York: Norton, 1950), p. 64.

9. The best we can hope for on such desperate occasions is what Gerard Manley Hopkins calls "Carrion Comfort," the consolation of death and decay. But even that cold comfort may have its compensation. We can think with Hopkins,

> That night, that year
> Of now done darkness I wretch lay wrestling with (my God!) my God.

The so-called "terrible sonnets" of Hopkins make the same point in each of a dozen different frightening and yet consoling ways. The opening lines alone say almost enough —

> No worst, there is none. Pitched past pitch of grief. . . .
> To seem the stranger lies my lot, my life. . . .
> I wake and feel the fell of dark, not day.
> Patience, hard thing! the hard thing but to pray. . . .
> My own heart let me more have pity on. . . .
> Thou art indeed just, Lord, if I contend. . . .

See *The Poems of Gerald Manley Hopkins*, pp. 99-103, 106-107.

10. See C. G. Jung, *The Archetypes of the Collective Unconscious*, trans. R. F. C. Hull, in *The Collected Works* (New York: Pantheon, 1959), IX:1, pp. 8-11.

11. The apocalyptic language of Romano Guardini's *The End of the Modern World* conveys the apposite images: "All the abysses of primeval ages yawn before man, all the wild choking growth of the long-dead forests presses forward from this second wilderness, all the monsters of the desert wastes, all the horrors of darkness are once more upon man. He stands again before chaos, a chaos more dreadful than the first because most men go their own complacent ways without seeing, because scientifically-educated gentlemen everywhere deliver their speeches as always, because the machines are running on schedule and because the authorities function as usual." It is important to know that Guardini is not a mere doom-sayer, however eloquent a one. He sees love disappearing "from the face of the public world," but alongside that grim fact the possibility that "man will come to experience this love anew, to taste the sovereignty of its origin, to know its independence of the world, to sense the mystery of its final *why*? Perhaps love will achieve an intimacy and harmony never known to this day." See Guardini, *The End of the Modern World*, trans. Joseph Theman and Herbert Burke (New York: Sheed & Ward, 1956), pp. 111-112, 132.

12. See Karl Barth, *Church Dogmatics*, trans. G. W. Bromiley (Edinburgh: T. & T. Clark, 1956), volume IV, Part I, pp. 259-272.

13. Our attitude, when we discover the nerve of failure, may be that of the holy fools of Russia, enshrined in the "pilgrim" books, *The Way of a Pilgrim* and *The Pilgrim Continues His Way*, or supremely translated into ironic theology by Erasmus, *In Praise of Folly*. It is also an attitude of confidence and willingness like that presented in the prayer attributed to Saint Francis of Assisi: "Lord, make me an instrument of your peace. Where there is hatred, let me show love; where there is injury, pardon; where there is doubt, faith; where there is despair, hope; where there is darkness, light, and where there is sadness, joy. O divine master, grant that I may not so much seek to be consoled as to console, to be understood as to understand, to be loved as to love. For it is in giving that we receive, it is in pardoning that we are pardoned, and it is in dying that we are born to eternal life."

14. There are many spiritual counselors available to help us meditate upon death, but few more witty or more wise than the figure of St. Augustine that Petrarch created as his dialogue-mate in the elaborate self-examination that

he called his *Secret*. In three dialogues, the fourteenth-century poet and humanist counsels himself — and us — in Augustine's voice. When Petrarch complains about living in "a state of suspense, always uncertain of the future," Augustine answers, or rather Petrarch answers himself, "placed as you are at the caprice of Fortune, you will be the only one of so many millions of mankind who shall live a life exempt from care!" Does he think about his failures, his weaknesses, his multiple faults? Shame is not the answer, Augustine says: "As Cicero tells us, it is but a poor thing to make shame do the work of reason. . . ." See what is good here on earth, what is positive, what is useful to prepare the way. And then, in the last dialogue, Augustine returns to the counsel of the first: "Think of Death, the fact so certain, the hour so uncertain, but everywhere and at all times imminent," for as he has said early on, "of all tremendous realities Death is the most tremendous." See *Petrarch's Secret*, trans. W. H. Draper (London: Chatto & Windus, 1911), pp. 94, 162-163, 32.

15. See S. L. Frank, *God With Us*, trans. Natalie Duddington (New Haven: Yale University Press, 1946), p. 143.

16. *Ibid*., p. 144. Frank sees our connection with all that *is* in these terms. In a later book, he puts it with a philosopher's elegance: "Reality in all the multiplicity of its manifestations is *life* in the widest sense of that term — a kind of immanent dynamism. Man's highest spiritual activity, the intensity of his intellectual, moral, artistic and religious strivings, the dark forces of passion that possess him, the unconscious elemental dynamism that interpenetrates the organic world, the physical energy throughout the universe, the terrible concentration of it that constitutes the nature of an atom — all these are manifestations of universal dynamism. . . . The same inexpressible principle which is the hidden transcendent essence of our inner being, and which we apprehend in the depths of our self as reality in contradistinction to the visible objective world, is at the same time the hidden basis of universal being as a whole." See S. L. Frank, *Reality and Man*, trans. Natalie Duddington (New York: Taplinger, 1965), p. 209.

CHAPTER EIGHT

1. Some of the traditional language of warning about sexual images is strong and is not so easy to throw off if one is impressed by it. Here, for example, is Peter Damian addressing young monks: "You are assailed by thick showers of all kinds of darts; the wicked spirits are gathered against you with all

the vices of the flesh, and they hurl down violent storms upon you. Wars rage in your very bones, and the furnace of your body belches forth balls of fire like restless Vesuvius or fiery Etna." See St. Peter Damian, *Selected Writings on the Spiritual Life*, trans. Patricia McNulty (New York: Harpers, 1959), p. 124.

2. The Song of Songs "calls a cheek a cheek, a breast a breast, and an eye an eye. But it also calls a cheek a piece of pomegranate, a breast a young roe, an eye a weapon that wounds, and brings up among the heavy artillery of love one hair on the neck." See Barry Ulanov, "The Song of Songs: The Rhetoric of Love," in *The Bridge: A Yearbook of Judaeo-Christian Studies*, Vol. IV (New York: Pantheon, 1962), p. 89. See also St. Bernard as quoted in it: "O love, so precipitate, so violent, so ardent, so impetuous, suffering the mind to entertain no thought but of thyself, spurning everything, despising everything which is not thyself, content with thyself alone!" From Bernard's *Sermons on the Canticle*, II, 435. The examples are almost endless, each vying with the others for intensity of feeling and voluptuousness of rhetoric.

3. See Boutauld, *The Art of Conversing with God*, pp. 24-25. See also St. John of the Cross, *Dark Night of the Soul*, in *The Complete Works*, I, pp. 330-331; Julian of Norwich, *The Revelations of Divine Love*, trans. James Walsh (New York: Harpers, 1961), p. 158; and Adriana Zarri, "Woman's Prayer and Man's Liturgy," in *Prayer and Community*, ed. Herman Schmidt (New York: Herder and Herder, 1970), pp. 85-86, for the quotations from Elizabeth of the Trinity.

4. "Batter my heart," No. XIV of Donne's Holy Sonnets, is the most adventurously sensual of the so-called Divine Poems, but by no means the only one to use human sexuality so directly. See, for example, No. XVIII of the Holy Sonnets, "Show me dear Christ, thy spouse, so bright and clear."

5. For a discussion of sexual feelings in prayer, see Ann Belford Ulanov, "What Do We Think People Are Doing When They Pray?," pp. 397-398.

6. According to Boehme, Sophia or Wisdom, the bride of the soul, "has revealed Herself in the precious Name JESUS as Christ the serpent-treader, as the anointed of God. She kisses [the soul] completely inwardly with her sweet love and presses love into its desire as a sign of victory. Here Adam according to his heavenly part is resurrected from the dead in Christ." The rhetoric is extravagant, but it also reflects Boehme's modesty; at this point, he says he can write no more, "for this is the marriage of the lamb when the noble pearl is sown with great triumph. . . ." See *The Way to Christ*, p. 45.

7. See *Mediaeval Netherlands Religious Literature*, trans. E. Colledge (New York: London House and Maxwell, 1965), pp. 8-9 , 17-29.

8. This is not to make a religion of the body but to make sure that in religion the body has its appropriate place, for we are, as Augustine never tires of reminding us, as much bodified spirits as we are inspirited bodies. We should not forget the exultant truth of Psalm 84: "My heart and my flesh crieth out for the living God," in the King James; "my heart and flesh sing for joy to the living God," in the Revised Standard Version.

9. Viktor Frankl, the noted existentialist and depth psychologist, distinguishes three levels of attraction in persons and their accompanying attitudes: "The most primitive attitude concerns itself with the outermost layer: this is the sexual attitude. The bodily appearance of the other person happens to be sexually arousing. . . .the erotically disposed person penetrates deeper than the one who is only sexually disposed . . . into the psychic structure of the other person. . . . we are also 'infatuated' with the other's psychic characteristics . . . stirred by the peculiar (but not the unique) psyche of the partner. . . . Loving . . . alone penetrates as deeply as possible into the personal structure of the partner. Loving represents a coming to relationship with another as a spiritual being." Viktor E. Frankl, *The Doctor and the Soul*, trans. Richard and Clara Winston (New York: Knopf, 1965), pp. 134-135.

10. For Vladimir Solovyev, the nineteenth-century Russian theologian, philosopher, and poet, sexual love at its highest in married love both reinforces our individuality as persons and joins us to the "all-oneness" of the "cosmic process." In such a union, "in the moment of sexual impulse . . . the inward unity or community with the 'other,' with the 'all,' receives its concrete embodiment in the relation to a single person of the other sex, who represents in itself this complementary 'all' in one." See Vladimir Solovyev, *The Meaning of Love*, trans. Jane Marshall (London: Geoffrey Bles, 1945), pp. 75-76.

11. For extended discussion of the opposite sex within ourselves, see Ann Belford Ulanov, *The Feminine in Jungian Psychology and in Christian Theology* (Evanston: Northwestern, 1971), pp. 35-45 and chapters 11 and 12. See also Ann Belford Ulanov, *Receiving Woman, Studies in the Psychology and Theology of the Feminine* (Philadelphia: Westminster Press, 1981), chapter 6.

12. See "God, love, and heaven," chapter 12 of Peter Geach's *Truth, Love and*

Immortality: An Introduction to McTaggart's Philosophy (Berkeley: University of California Press, 1979), and especially pp. 167-169.

13. See Ruysbroeck, *The Spiritual Espousals*, pp. 162-163.

14. See chapters 5 and 6 of Book III of *Gargantua and Pantagruel*, where Rabelais makes his case for mutual solace as at least as much the motivation for marriage as procreation. There his benevolent spokesman, Pantagruel, argues from the "law of Moses," paraphrasing those texts in Deuteronomy which clearly sanction his interpretation: "And what man *is there* that hath betrothed a wife, and hath not taken her? Let him go and return unto his house, lest he die in the battle, and another man take her" (20:7). "When a man hath taken a new wife, he shall not go out to war, neither shall he be charged with any business: *but* he shall be free at home one year, and shall cheer up his wife which he hath taken" (24:5). A good modern translation of Rabelais is that by J. M. Cohen (Baltimore: Penguin, 1955).

CHAPTER NINE

1. "There are many paths to the summit of Mount Fuji, say the Japanese; and there are many religions that lead to something or someone who lies in impenetrable darkness beyond the cloud of unknowing." Thus William Johnston in *Silent Music: The Science of Meditation* (New York: Harper & Row, 1975), p. 170. Our ecumenism in prayer may not extend to Mount Fuji, but it must surely gain from recognizing the range of our own interests and needs in prayer. These are sometimes immanentist in emphasis, sometimes transcendental, on occasion insistently directed to social and liturgical worship, often as firmly inner-directed, and always, one way or another, caught up in the world of others and otherness.

2. These words in Hebrews 7:25 emphasize the special quality of Jesus's eternal priesthood. In him, as in no other figure in any religion, the immanent and the transcendental are united; in his priestly role, he intercedes for us at every level and responds to everything that touches us, from the most trivial worldly anxiety to the most exalted other-worldly concern.

3. "Since prayer is a dialogue it is not the mind's fleeing far away from itself. Neither is it flight from the world. It gives the created being a new direction, but it does not withdraw from it. . . . the man who prays to God does not vanish in the clouds like Elijah; he remains here, and, in a sense, more concentrated than ever on the world. . . . He has not so much left it as turned a new gaze on it so that he now lives in it from within his and its source in

God." Nédoncelle, *The Nature and Use of Prayer*, p. 97. Adrian Stokes, the psychologically oriented critic and historian of art, suggests that in addition to living with the people of our world we also live with the inhabitants of our interiority: "the ceaseless operations in the primary process . . . which Kleinians especially call 'the inner life.' For them it revolves round the positions and relations of inner objects, includes envisagement of their strong corporeal character, a crowded scene. . . ." Adrian Stokes, *A Game That Must Be Lost* (Cheshire: Carcanet Press, 1973), p. 117.

4. Depth psychologists talk about such entanglements with others under the heading of projection; we cast onto the other person parts of ourselves we do not yet know or accept as our own. A piece of us then attaches to the other person and we feel overly preoccupied with and agitated by that person. For full discussion of the intricacies of these interactions and the attitude needed to resolve them, see Ann and Barry Ulanov, *Religion and the Unconscious*, pp. 220-239.

5. We can be instructed by the reverence Dante shows for such a figure as Brunetto Latini. With the implacable judgment that guides him throughout his allegory of the afterlife, he places him in the hell of the Sodomites, but he pauses to pay his full respects to his great teacher, and they are prayerful ones. If his prayers were fully answered, he tells Ser Brunetto, "you would not be banished from human nature, for in my memory is fixed, and now pierces my heart, the dear, kind, paternal image of you in the world, when hour by hour you taught me how man makes himself eternal. . . ." See Dante's *Inferno*, XV:79-85.

6. For a somewhat technical philosophical discussion of the "notion of causation acting backwards," see Anthony Kenny, *The God of the Philosophers* (Oxford: Clarendon Press, 1979), pp. 103-109. The difficulty with any argument in this area is that it in effect shortens the hand of God, taking small bits away from omnipotent being in the rigors of a human logic: "Of course, God will not, even if he can bring about the past, make undone what is done. . ." (106). This is precisely the kind of statement that makes philosophical necessity anathema to Lev Shestov (see above, p. 142).

7. We must be open in our prayers for the healing of others to share their pain and to share their recovery. We have the example of Jesus in the healing of Lazarus, as John tells the story (11:5-44). When Jesus sees Lazarus's sister Mary and his friends weeping over Lazarus, he is "deeply moved in spirit and troubled." He weeps. He brings Lazarus back with a full display of his feeling, no less important in the event than his miraculous intervention. "Belief in miracles," Bonhoeffer writes, "is belief in a visible epiphany.

Nothing happens in me if I assert my belief in miracles. There is only faith where a man so surrenders himself to the humiliated God-man as to stake his life on him, even when this seems against all sense." See Dietrich Bonhoeffer, *Christ the Center*, trans. John Bowden (New York: Harper & Row, 1966), pp. 114-115.

8. See Albrecht Goes, *The Burnt Offering*, trans. Michael Hamburger (New York: Pantheon, 1956).

9. "The mark of tragedy," says Ralph Harper, "is its reversal of everything one ordinarily takes for granted. . . . Tragedy is the suffering that convinces man that life is not to be taken for granted." See *The Path of Darkness* (Cleveland: Case Western Reserve University Press, 1968), pp. 39-40. "The soul should try to be ready to accept any suffering that God sends him," says Dom Eugene Boylan in the concluding paragraph of his *Difficulties in Mental Prayer*, "for union with Jesus is sealed in the fellowship of His sufferings and by our patient endurance we are made partakers of the Passion of Christ" (Westminster: Newman, 1963 [1943]), p. 123.

10. Few prayers have been prayed so constantly — incessantly, really — as the Jesus Prayer, the mantra of Eastern Christendom: "Lord Jesus Christ, Son of God, have mercy on me, a sinner." Its effectiveness has been attested to again and again by the saints, canonized or not, who have made its few words the basis of their mental prayer. See chapter 51, "On the Jesus Prayer," in *Unseen Warfare: The Spiritual Combat and Path to Paradise of Lorenzo Scupoli*, trans. from Theophan's Russian text by E. Kadloubovsky and G. E. H. Palmer (London: Faber, 1963), pp. 158-161.

11. Pauline theology hangs on this invitation to become another Christ. Everything in St. Paul's spirituality moves round the conviction that he lives in Christ, a reality that permeates his being. The classical statement is Gal. 2:20: "I have been crucified with Christ: it is no longer I who live, but Christ who lives in me; and the life I now live in the flesh I live by faith in the Son of God, who loved me and gave himself for me." The very modern-sounding statement that follows ("I do not nullify the grace of God") suggests the psychological balance and ease that Paul has found in living in Christ.

12. The principle is succinctly stated in Proverbs 27:10: "Better is a neighbor who is near than a brother who is far away." To be a good Samaritan is not a matter of heroic acts but of easy availability, to be as near to an act of kindness or of love, no matter how slight, as the words that well up in our heart. That is what prayer instructs us to do; that is how prayer instructs us to be

13. Eugene Boylan's summation of the meaning of the doctrine of the mystical body — the understanding that we are members one of another and all one in Christ — suggests the psychological enrichment that comes with the understanding: Christ "gives us His Father by making us sons of God; He gives us His Mother . . . to be our Mother also. . . . He gives us his own Spirit to vivify us with the newness and fullness of life. He gives us His own life. . . . . His merits . . . His innocence . . . His Flesh and Blood. . . . He gives us Himself, uniting us to Himself in such a way that, without losing our own personality, we 'put on Christ,' and can live and act and pray in His Name as indeed He lives and acts and prays in our name." See *Difficulties in Mental Prayer*, pp. 95-96.

14. Meister Eckhart has a wonderful sermon, "God Laughs and Plays," that captures the freedom that comes to us when we consent to the Spirit moving through us. See *Meister Eckhart*, trans. Raymond B. Blakney (New York: Harper, 1941), pp. 143-145.

CHAPTER TEN

1. See Boutauld, *The Art of Conversing with God*, p. 26.

2. The prayer in 2 Baruch (48:2-24), one of the four apocryphal writings that carry the name of the secretary to the prophet Jeremiah, connects us to the force that really can do all:

> Lord, you summon the times and they stand before you,
>> you dismiss the ages and they yield to you,
>> you arrange the seasons and they obey you,
> You alone know the duration of history. . . .
> You can measure fire, you can weigh the wind. . . .
> You instruct creation in your understanding. . . .

See Nicholas de Lange, *Apocrypha: Jewish Literature of the Hellenistic Age* (New York: Viking, 1978), pp. 220-221.

3. The superb conceit in so many of the poems of Charles Péguy is to speak in the voice of God, as for example in his "Vision of Prayer," where the Lord speaks to us after we have spoken to him:

> *Our Father who art in Heaven*. Of course when a man begins like that.
> When he says those three or four words to me.
> When he begins by making those three or four words move ahead of him.
> After that he can go on, he can tell me what he pleases.

Because, you understand, I am disarmed.
And my son knew it well.
My son who loved those men so very much.
Who had acquired a taste for them, and for the earth, and all that.

See *Basic Verities*, pp. 262-265.

4. Jung proposes a hypothesis about these moving coincidences. They demonstrate what he calls the principle of synchronicity which he defines as the subjectively significant concurrence of objective and subjective events that are not causally connected. In other words, the meaning is a meaning felt by the person involved. Jung suggests that this principle of synchronicity be added to the principles of space, time, and causality in our construction of the laws that govern reality. See C. G. Jung, "Synchronicity: An Acausal Connecting Principle," in *The Structure and Dynamics of the Psyche*, trans. R. F. C. Hull in *The Collected Works* (New York: Pantheon, 1960), VIII, pp. 417-532.

5. The depth psychologist Charles Odier discusses "magic thinking" at great length. Its meaning can be summed up as being motivated by wishes, needs, fears that lead to a confusion of inner state with outer reality, of self with other. It is as if thinking or feeling something is tantamount to making it so. See Charles Odier, *Anxiety and Magic Thinking*, trans. Marie-Louise Schoelly and Mary Jane Sherfey (New York: International Universities Press, 1956), pp. 63-64.

6. It is a discourse that flows easily into prayer. See for example the remarkable collection of prayers for life, health, and healing gathered together in chapter 5 of John Mbiti's *The Prayers of African Religion* (Maryknoll: Orbis Books, 1975), pp. 44-52. "It is remarkable how African peoples so confidently address spiritual realities," says Professor Mbiti. "In many of their prayers for healing, there is virtually no barrier between the realm of man and the spiritual realm. . . . Praying is not all worship; it is also rhetorical dialogue, a platform for man's questioning and heart-searching in the presence of God and the other spiritual realities" (44).

7. For discussion of this mode of knowing through identifying with the other who is known, see Ann Belford Ulanov, *Receiving Woman*, pp. 77-83.

8. "I need but to consider that I am able from moment to moment to draw my breath; to live by an act which is my very being, yet is not mine, for I do not breathe by choice or will, still less by my own devising; and then to consider what is more fully mine, my act of thought, an act which aspires to identify itself with the objective truth of things, to see all beings, and

myself among them, impartially, as from a great height, as though from the steps of a heavenly throne: My thought which is nevertheless momentary, precariously seated in a tremor of my cerebral nerves, and embodied in a trifling act of strung together words, or the imaged ghosts of words; when I see how much of being and of truth is somehow balanced on the absurd pin-point of my perishable moment, I step into the contemplation of him who does not alter or pass, who possesses and masters all he knows." See Austin Farrer, *The Glass of Vision* (Westminster: Dacre Press, 1948), pp. 96-97.

9. The writer in question is the Russian poet Osip Mandelstam, hated and sent to his death by Stalin because of a trivial passing remark about the dictator in one of his poems. His wife is Nadezhda Mandelstam, whose volumes *Hope Against Hope* and *Hope Abandoned*, translated by Max Hayward (New York: Atheneum, 1970 and 1974), not only memorialize the great poet but show us a long-lived woman of the same stature, a loving chronicler of the life of her husband, a discerning critic, a shrewd observer of events in her country and in our world. She is also a religious thinker: "We have all made small compromises and many, or rather the majority, have gone on to make major ones. . . . People were set free by Christianity but, having tasted freedom, they abandoned it and turned to atheism with its sprinkling of skeptical phrases and the pseudo-rational formulae of a pitiful humanism. There is a glaringly obvious connection between the loss of inner freedom and the abandonment of Christianity, but it escapes the blind and those who deliberately close their eyes. Yet this is the basic feature of our times and could not have been demonstrated more dramatically." See *Hope Abandoned*, pp. 581-582.

10. Such a light is the poet Gertrud Kolmar. Caught by the Nazi machine and unwilling to leave her aged father who would not seek escape, Kolmar remained in Germany. After the repeated horrors of the seizure of the family house, forced labor in a factory, and finally a train to the death camps, her death was inevitable. Indeed, it had long been visible on the horizon. She went on writing poetry despite all this and without any assurance her poems would survive her. Many of her poems were lost, but some were saved and published after her death. She says in a letter: "I seek, probably with insufficient strength, to create for eternity." See *Dark Soliloquy: The Selected Poems of Gertrud Kolmar*, trans. Henry A. Smith (New York: Seabury, 1975), p. 3.

11. "We do not know whom your grace has already blessed and transformed, among all those who seem to be far from you; we feel ourselves no better than those who think they are still groping in the darkness, than those whose

deeds, and therefore whose hearts, outwardly at least contradict your commandments," Karl Rahner prays. "It is, then, not our word but yours which is the last we can or will say of ourselves, the word of your grace." See Hugo and Karl Rahner, *Prayers for Meditation*, trans. Rosaleen Brennan (New York: Herder and Herder, 1963), pp. 42-43.

12. We should remember on these happy occasions, when we are caught up both in our awareness of God's presence and our awareness of our awareness, Pascal's insistence that "it is the heart, not reason, which experiences God. This then is faith: God perceived by the heart and not by reason." It is not that the experiences of the heart are lower than those of reason. "The heart has its reasons, of which reason knows nothing," is one of Pascal's properly famous *aperçus*. More straightforwardly, he says, "The heart has its own order; the intellect has its own, which is by way of principle and demonstration; the heart's is of a different kind. A claim to be loved is not proved by setting out in order the causes of loves; that would be ridiculous. Jesus Christ and St. Paul employ the method of charity, not of intellect. . . . St. Augustine likewise. This method consists chiefly in digressing upon every point that refers to the end, so as to keep it always in sight." See *Pascal's Pensées*, trans. John Warrington (London: Everyman, 1960), Fragments 225, 224, 575, pp. 59-60, 166-167.

13. The prayer continues —

> Kindle the hearts which, without Thee, are cold and dull:
> Enlighten the minds which, without Thee, are dark and blind.
> Fill the Church which, without Thee, is an empty shrine,
> And teach us to pray.

See *The One Who Listens: A Book of Prayer*, ed. M. Hollings and E. Gulick (New York: Morehouse-Barlow, 1971), p. 103.

14. See *Meister Eckhart*, p. 122. See also Henry Suso, *Little Book of Eternal Wisdom and Little Book of Truth*, trans. James M. Clark (London: Faber and Faber, 1953), p. 80; Simone Weil, *Waiting for God*, pp. 89, 107; and Ruysbroeck, *The Spiritual Espousals*, p. 190.

15. See Paul Ricoeur, *Freud and Philosophy: An Essay on Interpretation*, trans. Denis Savage (New Haven: Yale University Press, 1970), p. 549.

16. See Geach, *Truth, Love and Immortality*, p. 167.

17. There is no more concentrated or graceful presentation of *The Triple Way* than the brief treatise (or opusculum) of St. Bonaventure that goes by that

name and the subtitle, *or Love Enkindled*. See the translation by José de Vinck, in *The Works of Bonaventure* (Paterson: St. Anthony Guild Press, 1960), I, pp. 59-94.

18. We use the word "dialectical" here in a more-or-less Barthian sense, to suggest that the answer to prayer in the way of purgation is like that approach to God that will not accept any reduction to simple categories of Yes and No. Right and wrong, though they continue to exist for us, are seen in a new light, multifaceted, and free of crude all-encompassing judgments.

19. We should recognize with Mircea Eliade that the "history of religious meanings must always be regarded as forming part of the history of the human spirit," which is to say, whether speaking of East or West, those meanings are part of our sense of ourselves living in this world. More particularly, when we understand, as Eliade expects the historian of religions to do, "the permanence of what has been called man's specific existential situation of 'being in the world,'" we see that "the experience of the sacred is its correlate. In fact, man's becoming aware of his own mode of being and assuming his *presence* in the world together constitute a 'religious' experience." See Eliade, *The Quest: History and Meaning in Religion* (Chicago: University of Chicago Press, 1969), p. 9.

20. In *Our Savage God: The Perverse Use of Eastern Thought* (New York: Sheed & Ward, 1974), the late Spalding Professor of Comparative Religion at Oxford, R. C. Zaehner, gives us fair warning of what can happen when Eastern mysticism is taken up by Westerners ill-equipped to understand it. "You do not have to be a logician to see that any philosophy that asserts that 'justice *is* strife,' or that everything except the Absolute One does not in any meaningful sense exist, may result in such phenomena as Charles Manson, for whom killing and being killed were identical and the same. He is no doubt an exceptional case, but there have been other murderers since in California who have interpreted Eastern mysticism in just this way. Most people regret this, but there *is* a moral ambivalence both in Neo-Vedanta and Zen as there is in Heraclitus and Parmenides, and in our everyday world this ambivalence can have disastrous results" (p. 15). Zaehner's book is in one sense a screed, but it is also a profoundly moving meditation on our world, for him clearly ordained by the Creator-God of Christianity, which is both frightening and imbued with "the compassion of God crucified in Christ" (p. 305).

CHAPTER ELEVEN

1. Prayer of the heart is central to Orthodox spirituality, both Greek and Russian: "The heart governs and reigns over the whole bodily organism. . . . For there, in the heart, is the mind, and all the thoughts of the soul and its expectation; and in this way grace penetrates also to all the members of the body. . . . Within the heart are unfathomable depths. There are reception rooms and bedchambers in it, doors and porches. . . . The heart is Christ's palace. . . ." The Homilies of St. Makarios, quoted in Igumen Chariton, *The Art of Prayer*, p. 18. See also other indexed references to the heart in that volume and the crucial collection, *Writings from the Philokalia on Prayer of the Heart*, trans. E. Kadloubovsky and G. E. H. Palmer (London: Faber, 1951), *passim*.

2. The transfiguration is a more celebrated devotion in Eastern Christianity than it is in the West. But the reiteration of images of interior burning and inner light in the spiritual writing of the West shows how captivating the language of transfiguration is for all of us. We should be mindful here not only of the New Testament texts which picture the transfigured Christ (Matt. 17:1-13, Mark 9:2-13, Luke 9:28-36) but also the prefigurations of the event in the Old Testament in the enthronement of Yahweh and in the figures of Moses and Elijah, who appear with Jesus in the transfiguration texts.

3. We come by fits and starts to the higher graces of prayer. As the seventeenth-century spiritual writer Louis Lallemant reminds us, "In vain do we labour to have this sense of the presence of God unless he himself bestows it upon us." We discover that "Meditation wearies and fatigues the mind, and [that] its acts are of short duration. . . ." But we also find, to our delight, that "those of contemplation, even such as is of a common order, last whole hours without labour and without weariness. . . ." Contemplation can then become nothing less than "a participation in the state of glory." See *The Spiritual Doctrine of Father Louis Lallemant*, ed. A. G. McDougall (Westminster: Newman Press, 1955 [1928]), pp. 259, 261-262.

4. The text is from Revelations 3:20. Of this kind of invitation to the life of prayer, Jacques and Raissa Maritain say, "This is the call of love, to which nothing but love can reply." See *Prayer and Intelligence* (New York: Sheed & Ward, 1943), p. 11.

5. We should neither be too quick to accept nor to condemn these remarkable performers in the mystical life. Herbert Thurston, an indefatigable investigator of such people, cautions us in summing up the case of Margery Kempe, that startling contemporary of Julian of Norwich who was either

gifted or plagued with endless weeping: "The problem which confronts us in case after case of these queer mystics is the combination of pronounced hysteria with a genuine love of God, great generosity and self-sacrifice, unflinching courage, and very often the occurrence of strange psychic phenomena, particularly in the form of a knowledge of distant and future events." See Herbert Thurston, *Surprising Mystics* (Chicago: Regnery, 1955), p. 36.

6. At such moments, when we feel our senses stretched beyond ordinary use, we should remember the great medieval testimonies to the senses as talismans of the Lord, each one gifted to take in some part of the mystery of creation. Solomon Ibn Gabirol is a moving example in that medieval Hebrew masterpiece, the long devotional poem called *The Kingly Crown:*

> Who can know the secret of Thine accomplishments, when Thou madest for
> the body the means for Thy work?
> Thou gavest him eyes to see Thy signs,
> Ears, to hear Thy wonders,
> Mind, to grasp some part of Thy mystery,
> Mouth, to tell Thy praise,
> Tongue, to relate Thy mighty deeds to every comer,
> As I do to-day, I Thy servant, the son of Thy handmaid,
> I tell, according to the shortness of my tongue, one tiny part of Thy greatness.

See the translation by Bernard Lewis (London: Vallentine Mitchell, 1961), p. 51.

7. See St. Teresa, *Conceptions of the Love of God*, Ch. IV, in *The Complete Works of St. Teresa*, II, pp. 383-387.

8. It is precisely the image of Jacob's ladder that Nicolete Gray uses for her lovely "Bible Picture Book from Anglo-Saxon and 12th Century English Mss." In her Foreward she answers those who might wonder about offering children an allegorical conception of the Bible: "But surely it appeals to just that instinct which leads children to seek knowledge and expression through make-believe and play-acting. What is an allegory but a play where everybody knows that the actors represent something like, but other than themselves?" See *Jacob's Ladder* (London: Faber, 1949), p. 9. The Preface to the Commentary on the Song of Songs attributed to Gregory the Great makes the point very clear: "For allegory serves as a kind of machine to the spirit by means of which it may be raised up to God. Thus when enigmas are set before a man and he recognizes certain things in the words which are familiar to him, he may understand in the sense of the words what is not familiar to him; and by means of earthly words he is separated from earth. Since he does

not abhor what he knows, he may come to understand what he does not know. For the things which are known to us from which allegory is made are clothed in divine doctrine, and, when we recognize the thing by an exterior word, we may come to an interior understanding." See "The Aesthetics of Figurative Expression," in D. W. Robertson, Jr., *A Preface to Chaucer: Studies in Medieval Perspectives* (Princeton: Princeton University Press, 1962), pp. 52-64. The quotation appears on pp. 57-58 of this splendid compendium of information and interpretation.

9. Jung calls this greater subject "the Self." As "psychic totality," it "has a conscious as well as an unconscious aspect. Empirically, the self appears in dreams, myths, and fairytales in the figure of the 'supraordinate personality' . . . such as a king, hero, prophet, saviour, etc., or in the form of a totality symbol, such as the circle. . . . When it represents a . . . union of opposites, it can also appear as a united duality, in the form, for instance, of *tao* as the interplay of *yang* and *yin*, or of the hostile brothers, or of the hero and his adversary (arch-enemy, dragon), Faust and Mephistopheles, etc." C. G. Jung, *Psychological Types*, trans. R. F. C. Hull, in *The Collected Works* (Princeton: Princeton University Press, 1971), VI, p. 460.

10. See Jan Van Ruysbroeck, "The Book of the Sparkling Stone," in *Mediaeval Netherlands Literature*, p. 95; see also C. G. Jung, *Psychology and Alchemy*, trans. R. F. C. Hull in *The Collected Works* (New York: Pantheon, 1953), XII, p. 340.

11. The Prayer of Oblation from *The Book of Common Prayer* (1928 version) reads: "Wherefore O Lord and heavenly Father, according to the institution of thy dearly beloved Son our Saviour Jesus Christ, we, thy humble servants, do celebrate and make here before thy Divine Majesty, with these thy holy gifts, which we now offer unto thee, the memorial thy Son hath commanded us to make; having in remembrance his blessed passion and precious death, his mighty resurrection and glorious ascension; rendering unto thee most hearty thanks for the innumerable benefits procured unto us by the same." The Prayer of Invocation continues the offering: "And here we offer and present unto thee, O Lord, our selves, our souls and bodies, to be a reasonable, holy, and living sacrifice unto thee. . . ." See *The Book of Common Prayer* (New York: Oxford University Press, 1944), pp. 80-81.

12. According to Kant, this (absolute beginnings) is the nature of human freedom, where we find our spontaneity and our "power of self-determination." See *Immanuel Kant's Critique of Pure Reason*, trans. Norman Kemp Smith (London: Macmillan, 1953 [1929]), p. 464-465.

13. The first quotation is from Julian of Norwich, *The Revelations of Divine Love*, p. 209. The second quotation is from *Rule for A New Brother*, p. 6.

14. "Do the great lovers of God who turn to the Song of Songs do so merely to use the rhetoric of love? No, they are drawn to it because it is the very source of that rhetoric. Without it, they would be mute." Barry Ulanov, "The Song of Songs: The Rhetoric of Love," in *The Bridge*, IV, p. 118.

15. See Anthony Bloom, *Beginning to Pray*, p. 57.

16. The famous circle is attributed to many sources, reaching back at least as far as St. Augustine. Pascal's statement of it is as succinct as any and well enough known: "Reality is an infinite sphere, whose center is everywhere and whose circumference is nowhere. In short, the greatest sensible indication of God's omnipotence is the fact that human imagination loses itself in that thought." See the *Pensées*, fragment 390, p. 106.

17. See Paul Ricoeur, "On Consolation," in Alasdair MacIntyre and Paul Ricoeur, *The Religious Significance of Atheism* (New York: Columbia University Press, 1969), pp. 93-94, 98.

18. See D. W. Winnicott, *The Piggle: An Account of the Psychoanalytic Treatment of a Little Girl*, ed. Ishak Ramzy (New York: International Universities Press, 1977), pp. 55, 77, 139.

19. Cited in *The Soul Afire*, p. 298. See also Cuthbert Butler, *Western Mysticism* (New York: Harpers, 1966), p. 109.

20. Cited by J. Arintero, *Stages in Prayer*, p. 89n.

21. Etienne Gilson summarizes the higher degrees of love as presented in the last part of St. Bernard's *De diligendo Deo* (On the Love of God): "By dint of turning to God out of need, the soul soon begins to feel that to live with God is sweet: then she begins to love Him for Himself, yet without ceasing to love Him still for herself; so that she hesitates, alternating between a pure love and a self-interested cupidity, well-ordered though it be. It is in this state that the soul remains for the longest time, nor indeed can she ever wholly emerge from it in this life. To pass altogether beyond this mixture of cupidity and disinterested love and to rise to pure love of God, would be to pass out of this life and to live already the life of the blessed in heaven." See Gilson, *The Mystical Theology of Saint Bernard*, trans. A. H. C. Downes (London: Sheed & Ward, 1955 [1940]), p. 88.